mentor manager

mentor parent

How to Develop Responsible People and Build
Successful Relationships at Work and at Home

Linda Culp Dowling
Cecile Culp Mielenz, Ph.D.

ComCon Books

Mentor Manger, Mentor Parent

Printed in the United States of America

Library of Congress Control Number: 2002093605

ISBN: 0-9722782-4-9

ComCon Books

904 Cimarron Circle
Burneyville, OK 73430

888-606-7130
www.mentormanagermentorparent.com

DEDICATION

We dedicate this book to the memory of our grandmother, Nelle Hoyle Culp, and to our children Lisa, Laura, Jennifer, and Christine. Through them the threads of our heritage are becoming the tapestry of our future.

When we visited our grandmother, she enjoyed sharing our favorite foods and activities. She introduced us to flowers from the garden and coffee in china cups. She had all the time in the world for us, looked forward not backward, and enjoyed each day to its fullest.

When our children sit in the kitchen to talk, call for advice or a laugh, share time in the garden, or see humor in the ordinary, we delight in their presence, celebrate our lives' dearest relationships, and watch the tapestry unfold.

TABLE OF CONTENTS

CHAPTER FOUR - 132
Conferencing

CHAPTER FIVE - 182
Letting Go

ABOUT THE AUTHORS - 234

ACKNOWLEDGMENTS

We are grateful to the many people who have been part of our journey in writing this book. Our clients over the years have helped us learn the secrets of effective managers and parents. Many friends and associates read the early drafts of the book and gave us valuable feedback. Others graciously offered us use of their inspirational retreats for our writing: thank you to Mare, Kristi, Candy, Corinne and Al, Gayle and Wayne, Meredith and John, and Lucy and Patrick. Our publicists, Phenix & Phenix, expertly guided us through every step of the process. Through it all, our families provided a great deal of support, and we deeply appreciate their encouragement and confidence. To our husbands, Pete and Mike, we are especially grateful.

PREFACE

At a family reunion in March 1996, we reminisced about growing up together as cousins in central Oklahoma in the 1950s. Sharing personal stories and professional experiences, we discovered interesting parallels between Linda's observations as a management coach and Cecile's as a parent educator.

Linda told how her clients applied management skills with their children. A mother used coaching skills to help her daughter get to school on time. In a training session on discipline, a father realized that his own unclear expectations and inconsistency fueled his son's disobedience.

Cecile described several parents who discovered that methods for encouraging children also apply at work. A father who completed a series of parenting classes soon was promoted to president of his company because of his new techniques for working with people.

We found that both managers and parents feel a deep sense of responsibility for the actions of their employees and children. They share the same challenges and frustrations, even though managers have professional relationships with adults and parents have personal relationships with children. When faced with problem behavior, managers and parents often struggle to control their employees and children. However, the most effective managers and parents move beyond their concern about control and focus instead on encouraging responsibility and building relationships.

Drawing on our experiences, we created a model of strategies and skills designed to help our clients develop mentoring relationships rather than those based on control. *Mentor Manager, Mentor Parent* teaches managers and parents how to apply these proven techniques at work and at home.

Throughout the book, each of us shares true anecdotes about managers and parents, identified with our initials. While most of the anecdotes illustrate constructive behavior, some describe behavior that blocks effective communication. To protect the privacy of our clients, we have changed the names and circumstances of those involved. In addition, we have alternated genders to avoid stereotypes.

Learning from each other has deepened our relationship both personally and professionally. From our collaboration come these strategies to strengthen your relationships, as you become a mentor manager/mentor parent.

Linda Culp Dowling and Cecile Culp Mielenz

CHAPTER ONE

Control Styles of Managers and Parents

Every time your employee or child fails to do what you expect, you face a dilemma about control. What do you say to an employee who makes the same data entry errors again and again or spends too much time on personal phone calls? How do you deal with a toddler who throws a tantrum in the grocery store or a teenager who stays out too late? How can you control their behavior?

If you raise your voice, demand obedience, or dictate rules, employees and children resent your telling them what to do. The more they refuse to comply, the more frustrated you become and the harder you try to control.

Sometimes, you promise rewards or threaten punishment. You offer a bonus to an employee to make him sell more or a cookie to a dawdling child to make her get in the car. You threaten employees with overtime when they do not meet schedules, or you refuse to read a story to a child who will not go to bed. However, employees and children soon challenge your threats and promises with *If I finish early do I get to go home?* Or, *Do I get two stories if I get ready for bed fast?*

When all else fails, you may sidestep a fight and allow employees and children to do what they want. Telling an unsatisfactory employee that he does good work preempts his argument about required improvements. Letting a child watch one more TV show puts off a confrontation about bedtime. Yet, when you give in, employees and children perceive that rules have no meaning and do not apply to them.

When you demand, bribe, or give in, you begin a continuous cycle. The resulting resentment, challenge, and disrespect from your employees or children intensify your desire to control their behavior. Understanding how you perpetuate this cycle is the first step toward developing responsible people and building successful relationships at work and at home.

DETERMINING YOUR CONTROL STYLE

Before you discover new strategies to help you move beyond control, assess and understand how you currently respond in control situations with employees and children. Following are two self-tests, one for work and one for home. Take both tests now to reveal your control style.

SELF-TEST FOR WORK

For each situation, rank the responses according to the answers you are most likely to give, not necessarily what you think is the "best" answer:

- Use 4 to rank your *most* likely response.
- Use 3 to rank your next most likely response.
- Use 2 to rank your next most likely response.
- Use 1 to rank your *least* likely response.

Write a number in every blank. Use 4, 3, 2, and 1 for each situation. If the work situations are not familiar to you, rank the responses in the order that initially seems most like what you would say.

1.

You are the manager of a research laboratory funded by a granting agency that values efficiency. A new researcher, with experience at another lab, takes too much time processing experiments. What would you say to this new researcher?

____ a Your performance evaluation will be based on how fast you work.

____ b The granting agency expects us to finish five experiments a week. Would it help you if I finished up a few of yours?

____ c Finish that experiment today.

____ d Our grants depend on completing five experiments a week, so you need to work quickly.

2.

You are a radio station sales manager and require weekly sales reports from each salesperson. Their reports are all due today. What do you say to your new salesperson?

____ a I'll give you a few weeks to get used to the routine before you begin turning in sales reports.

____ b Have your sales report on my desk by five o'clock.

____ c You can't leave until you've turned in your report.

____ d Turn in your sales report each Friday so that I can calculate our total sales.

3.

Your administrative assistant is away for a two-week vacation. The temporary assistant gives you an outgoing letter for your signature. You notice that it contains two typos. What do you say to the temp?

____ a   If you'll correct this and get it right back to me, you can leave a little early for lunch.

____ b   This will be all right for today.

____ c   Letters reflect our company. Be sure they have no typos before you give them to me.

____ d   Please correct this letter.

4.

You are the head teller in a bank. You expect the tellers to schedule their lunch hours cooperatively so that everyone gets a lunch. One of your tellers insists on taking her lunch whenever she wants. What do you say to this teller?

____ a   I would really appreciate it if you would check with the other tellers before you schedule your lunch.

____ b   On some days not everyone is getting a full lunch hour. What is your perspective on this?

____ c   Take your lunch at eleven o'clock.

____ d   When do you need to go? Just let me know, and I'll fill in.

5.

You are the manager of a sporting goods store that provides uniforms for all local sports organizations. One of your employees comes to you with a Little League team's request for jerseys that you do not have in stock. What do you say to this employee?

____ a   Go ahead and special order them from Acme.

____ b   We'll probably have to special order them. Just leave it on my desk, and I'll do it.

____ c   If you want to become floor supervisor, I need to see you make these decisions yourself.

____ d   Always special order anything we don't have in stock. How can you get the best price and fastest delivery?

6.

You are a supervisor in a manufacturing plant. A machine operator produces an excessive number of rejected items, which have to be scrapped. What do you say to this employee?

____ a I know you're doing your best. Do you think it could be the machine? Let me try calibrating it.

____ b The quality of your work has to improve.

____ c Product quality must be consistent. How can you reduce your amount of scrap?

____ d Too much scrap makes us look bad to the plant manager.

7.

You are the branch manager of a library that has just changed computer programs. A librarian complains that there was nothing wrong with the old system. What do you say to the librarian?

____ a Changing to a new system is difficult. What is giving you the most trouble?

____ b Will you go to the training session Friday morning? If you'll do that, you can have Friday afternoon off.

____ c Don't complain. It's changed now.

____ d You're right, but they didn't ask us.

8.

You are a project manager in an engineering firm. An engineer tells you the client changes his mind so often that the project is going to run over budget. What do you say to your engineer?

____ a Let's talk about it. What kinds of changes does he want?

____ b Just do what you need to do, and I'll take the heat.

____ c If you can keep the costs down on this project, we'll have money for bonuses.

____ d Just tell him we can't make any more changes.

9.

You are the grocery store manager. Several of your customers have complained about spoiled produce. What do you say to the produce manager?

____ a Some customers are going to complain no matter what we do.

____ b I don't want to hear any more customer complaints about produce problems.

____ c Give me some ideas about what we could do to keep the produce fresh.

____ d Just get rid of any spoiled produce.

10.

You are the principal of an elementary school. A teacher refused to attend an after-school staff meeting to finalize the details for a school celebration. The next day she wants the plans changed. How might you respond to her?

_____ a   Don't come to me. You weren't at the meeting.

_____ b   If you can just let this one go, I'll put you in charge of the next celebration.

_____ c   I'm sorry you weren't there to help finalize the plans.

_____ d   I really like your ideas, but that's what the group decided.

11.

You are the manager of an insurance telemarketing center. You have an employee who wears mismatched, stained clothes to work. He has applied for a promotion that involves meeting the public and dressing more professionally. You have discussed this with him. On the day of his interview he dresses inappropriately. What do you say to him?

_____ a   Would you like to borrow my sport coat?

_____ b   If you want my support for this promotion, you had better change your clothes.

_____ c   Go home and change clothes before your interview.

_____ d   (You choose to say nothing to him about his attire.)

12.

You are the manager of a clinic that opens at eight each morning. Yet, the salaried bookkeeper typically arrives five to ten minutes late. As a result, she frequently must stay past five o'clock to complete her work. What do you say to the bookkeeper?

_____ a   If you don't get to work on time, I'll have to write you up.

_____ b   Get your act together and get to work on time.

_____ c   It's five o'clock. Don't worry about it. Go on home.

_____ d   (You choose to say nothing to her about her arrival and departure times.)

SELF-TEST FOR HOME

For each situation, rank the responses according to the answers you are most likely to give, not necessarily what you think is the "best" answer:

- Use 4 to rank your *most* likely response.
- Use 3 to rank your next most likely response.
- Use 2 to rank your next most likely response.
- Use 1 to rank your *least* likely response.

Write a number in every blank. Use 4, 3, 2, and 1 for each situation. If the situations do not reflect your children's ages, rank the responses in the order that initially seems most like what you would say.

1.

It's dinnertime. You want your two-year-old to wash his hands. What do you say?

4 a   You have to wash your hands if you want dinner.
1 b   Do you want to wash your hands?
2 c   Go wash your hands.
3 d   Before we eat dinner, we all wash our hands. I'll go with you.

2.

Your eight-year-old daughter wants to be responsible for feeding the dog and agrees to feed him every day when she comes home from school. Today, she walks in the door and turns on the TV. You notice the dog dish is empty. What do you say to her?

1 a   I know it's your favorite show, so I'll feed the dog this time.
3 b   Turn off the TV, and feed the dog.
2 c   If you don't feed the dog, you can't watch TV.
4 d   After you feed the dog, then you can watch TV.

3.

Your sixteen-year-old son has just received his driver's license. He returned the family car on time but did not return the keys to the hook by the door. What do you say to him?

2 a   I can't let you drive the car if you can't remember to put the keys back where they belong.
3 b   I can't find the keys. Do you know where they might be?
4 c   Thanks for bringing the car back on time. Always put the keys on the hook by the door so that the next person can find them.
1 d   It's my car, and I want the keys returned to the hook by the door.

7

4.

Your five-year-old son is learning how to make his bed. You observe him pulling up the blanket and bedspread, ignoring the rumpled sheets. What do you say to him?

____ a Do it the way I showed you, and I will be proud.

____ b The sheets are still at the foot of the bed. How can you fix that?

____ c You didn't pull up the sheet.

____ d You are doing such a good job of making your bed.

5.

Your thirteen-year-old daughter's responsibility is to set the table for dinner. The meal is ready, and she continues to talk to a friend on the phone. What do you say to your daughter?

____ a Put down the phone and set the table.

____ b Don't interrupt your conversation. I can manage it.

____ c You're going to be grounded unless you get off the phone and set the table.

____ d Dinner is ready now. How quickly can you set the table?

6.

You are getting ready to make an important telephone call and you anticipate that your seven-year-old son is likely to interrupt. What do you say to him?

____ a I'll just wait to make my phone call later.

____ b Don't interrupt me while I'm on the phone.

____ c I need to be on the phone for a few minutes. How can you keep busy until I'm through?

____ d If you don't interrupt me while I'm on the phone you can have animal crackers when I'm through.

7.

Your seventeen-year-old daughter needs a dress for the prom. You give her money to buy a dress. She comes home with not only the dress but with three other items. What do you say to your daughter?

____ a Show me everything you bought.

____ b It looks like I can never trust you to go shopping by yourself again.

____ c Take all of that other stuff back. I told you just to get a dress.

____ d I'm sure you will look beautiful in everything you bought.

8.

Your three-year-old son's playmate comes to you crying with a red welt under his eye. What do you say to your son?

___ a   What happened here?

___ b   Are you okay? Do you want your friend to go home?

___ c   If you can't be nice to your friends, you can't have them over.

___ d   Don't hurt your friends!

9.

Your eleven-year-old comes home from school and angrily declares, "My teacher yelled at me!" What do you say in response?

___ a   She had no right to yell at you!

___ b   You have to learn how to get along with her so that you'll pass the class.

___ c   How embarrassing! Tell me about it.

___ d   Don't do things that make her mad.

10.

Your eighteen-year-old son brings home a note from the wrestling coach stating that he cannot compete in an upcoming match because he has a pierced navel. What do you say to your son?

___ a   Get that out of your navel, and get ready to wrestle.

___ b   If you are not in that wrestling competition, you won't get on a college team.

___ c   I know you enjoyed wrestling. That must have been a hard choice.

___ d   Don't worry about it. I'll talk to him, and you'll get to wrestle.

11.

Your twelve-year-old daughter is responsible for doing her own laundry. As she is getting ready for school, she comes to you in tears because her favorite jeans are dirty. What do you say in response?

___ a   I'll wash them for you and bring them to school when they're dry.

___ b   If you can't keep those expensive jeans clean, I won't buy you any more.

___ c   If you had washed your clothes on the weekend like I told you, you wouldn't have that problem now.

___ d   That's disappointing. Those are your favorite jeans.

12.

Your four-year-old's bedtime is eight o'clock. It's twenty minutes after eight, and he is in his bed in the dark singing. How do you respond?

___ a   If you go to sleep now, I'll have a surprise for you in the morning.

___ b   Be quiet and go to sleep.

___ c   Can't you sleep? Just come and watch TV with me.

___ d   (You choose to say nothing to him.)

SCORING THE WORK SELF-TEST

On this page record your scores from the work self-test. For each item, enter the ranks you assigned to every letter. Add your scores vertically to determine your control style.

> ## NOTE THAT LETTERS ARE NO LONGER IN ALPHABETICAL ORDER.

1.	c ____	a ____	b ____	d ____
2.	b ____	c ____	a ____	d ____
3.	d ____	a ____	b ____	c ____
4.	c ____	a ____	d ____	b ____
5.	a ____	c ____	b ____	d ____
6.	b ____	d ____	a ____	c ____
7.	c ____	b ____	d ____	a ____
8.	d ____	c ____	b ____	a ____
9.	d ____	b ____	a ____	c ____
10.	a ____	b ____	d ____	c ____
11.	c ____	b ____	a ____	d ____
12.	b ____	a ____	c ____	d ____
TOTALS	____	____	____	____
	BOSS	MANIPULATOR	MARTYR	MENTOR

Circle your highest total score on the work self-test. Your highest score represents your primary control style at work.

SCORING THE HOME SELF-TEST

On this page record your scores from the home self-test. For each item, enter the ranks you assigned to every letter. Add your scores vertically to determine your control style.

NOTE THAT LETTERS ARE NO LONGER IN ALPHABETICAL ORDER.

1.	c 2	a 4	b 1	d 3
2.	b 3	c 2	a 1	d 4
3.	d 1	a 2	b 3	c 4
4.	c 2	a 1	d 4	b 3
5.	a 3	c 1	b 2	d 4
6.	b 2	d 1	a 3	c 4
7.	c 2	b 1	d 3	a 4
8.	d 1	c 3	b 2	a 4
9.	d 2	b 3	a 1	c 4
10.	a 2	b 3	d 1	c 4
11.	c 4	b 1	a 2	d 3
12.	b 3	a 1	c 2	d 4
TOTALS	27	23	25	45
	BOSS	MANIPULATOR	MARTYR	MENTOR

Circle your highest total score on the home self-test. Your highest score represents your primary control style at home.

The self-tests assess the extent of your reliance on four control styles: boss, manipulator, martyr, and mentor. Each style demonstrates a unique approach to the use of control.

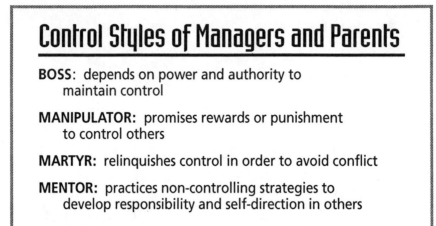

Control Styles of Managers and Parents

BOSS: depends on power and authority to maintain control

MANIPULATOR: promises rewards or punishment to control others

MARTYR: relinquishes control in order to avoid conflict

MENTOR: practices non-controlling strategies to develop responsibility and self-direction in others

Your scores identify your control style. A high score indicates a style that you use frequently; a low score represents a style that you rarely choose. You may discover that you rely on more than one style or that your work and home control styles differ.

If you score highest in the **mentor** column, look at your second highest score. You may have selected mentor answers because they appeared to be the obvious or best choices. In this case, your second highest score may more accurately describe your true style.

Your control style may originate in the powerful influence of your role models. Perhaps you imitate your first manager or recognize the similarity to a parent when you speak or gesture. If your role model is a mentor, mentoring skills will seem natural to you. On the other hand, if your role model is a boss, manipulator, or martyr, you may find yourself reverting to those familiar patterns, especially when you are under stress or time pressure. Whether you imitate a role model or consciously choose to behave differently, your control style reflects your underlying assumptions about relationships with employees and children.

THE BOSS

The boss believes that others will not act appropriately unless she tells them what to do. She does not give them credit for their knowledge or skills, nor does she consider their personal motivation. Her approach relies on the power of her position to demand the behavior she wants. Expecting compliance, the boss says *Do that!* Her disrespectful style stifles initiative in her employees and children, who learn to wait passively for instructions. The boss fosters resentment in others, particularly those who possess experience and motivation of their own.

The Boss at Work

The boss takes advantage of his authority to control the workplace. He disregards others and makes choices for them with a manner that implies *Don't challenge me.* The boss contends *I have to tell them everything*, while employees complain *He treats us like children* and avoid him. Competent employees especially resent his style of leadership.

> *Vernetta, a social services supervisor, came to me for assistance. She sheepishly acknowledged that she was embarrassed by comments from her employees. "When I come into the room, my employees say, 'We don't have to think anymore now that she's here.'"*
>
> —*L.C.D.*

Unfortunately, today's pace and pressure encourage the boss's need for immediate compliance. Accustomed to quick responses from pagers and e-mail, he expects employees to perform without delay. *I need this now.* Or, *Handle this right away.* Although his demands gain short-term results, he frustrates his employees and exhausts himself.

Nita, a dean at a large midwestern college, asked me to lead a retreat for all the secretaries in the college. "I want the secretaries to understand that they must drop everything when my office calls," she explained to me.

Imagining myself in a busy one-secretary department with students, faculty, and an administrator all wanting my attention, I asked her, "How do the secretaries feel about your demand for their immediate compliance?"

"How should I know?" Nita responded.

—L.C.D.

The boss rarely takes time to listen to others' ideas. Sometimes, he gives lip service to participative management or team involvement, only to dominate department meetings and ignore established teams. He believes that he has all the answers and implements new ideas without consulting others. Independently, he may rewrite job descriptions, create rules and systems, or design forms and procedures. He insists on authorizing every expense and approving every change, stifling employees' participation and initiative.

Stanton's health club employees suggested that the club add two more treadmills, offer protein shakes at the snack bar, and include a free guest pass in each monthly newsletter. Yet, Stanton quickly rejected their ideas. He justified his response with, "Their ideas are never any good. I told them my door was always open, but they only suggest things that won't work or that we've tried before."

—L.C.D.

The authoritarian approach can exist at all management levels. However, a lack of skill, self-confidence, or experience can increase a manager's dependence on this style. The new manager with low managerial maturity often assumes *My job is to assign their work,* overlooking his duty to develop responsible and self-directed people.

The Boss at Home

The boss parent uses power to control the child, assuming *I'm the parent. That's my job.* She expects compliance when she says *Get in the car, Eat your dinner,* or *Turn off the TV.* If necessary, she tries a more forceful statement, *I told you to get in the car!* The boss may even resort to physical power by placing the child in the car or turning off the television.

> *Jiana came into the counseling office seeking advice about her twelve-year-old son, Darian. "Do you think Darian should take swimming lessons this summer for three or five days each week?"*
>
> *When I asked about Darian's opinion, Jiana replied, "Don't you think that a little boy should just do what his mother tells him?"*
>
> — C.C.M.

When the parent orders *Do that!* she expects the child to comply simply in response to her mandate. Without understanding any other reason, he fails to learn how to make responsible choices in the future. Eventually, the child can lose initiative and motivation. If he already knows what to do, the child resents her authoritarian approach that does not give him credit for thinking.

When the boss focuses on compliance, she diminishes the individuality of the child. When she says *Get in the car,* she could be addressing any child. If the child has thoughts or feelings about the demand, the parent appears not to hear them. Because the child does not feel valued and respected, he treats his parent with disrespect in return. *I'm not getting in the car, and you can't make me!*

> *Sixteen-year-old Samuel planned to take his girlfriend to a movie on Saturday night. His father, Douglas, told Samuel to wash the car before going. Saturday afternoon the girlfriend called to say that she had to attend an evening function with her parents and would prefer to go to the two o'clock matinee.*

Although Douglas was not home to approve, Samuel decided he would wash the car after the matinee. Douglas was waiting for Samuel when he returned at five o'clock. He grabbed the keys from Samuel's hand and yelled, "I told you to wash that car first!"

Samuel walked away muttering, "I hate you!"

— *C.C.M.*

Your Use of The Boss Style

If you have a high score in the boss category on either self-test, you concentrate on controlling the behavior of others. You may gain compliance because of your dominance, but beware! Without the opportunity to solve their own problems, your employees and children will not develop the skills to make self-directed decisions. Your demanding manner will hinder meaningful relationships. When you model disrespect, others will respond to you in kind.

On the following journal page, record words and phrases you say during the next few days that suggest the boss control style.

CONTROL STYLE JOURNAL: BOSS

Jot down words and phrases you say at **WORK** that suggest
the **boss** control style.

_____

_____

_____

_____

_____

_____

_____

_____

Jot down words and phrases you say at **HOME** that suggest
the **boss** control style.

_____

_____

_____

_____

_____

_____

_____

_____

THE MANIPULATOR

Like the boss, the manipulator believes that his employees and children will not act appropriately without his intervention. Although he gives them credit for their knowledge or skills, he does not believe in their personal motivation. While the boss says *Do that!* the manipulator says *If you'll do that, I'll give you this!* He promises rewards, punishments, contingencies, and consequences. Eventually, his relationships revolve around searching for the unique reward or particular punishment to motivate behavior.

The Manipulator at Work

The manipulator discounts the possibility that personal satisfaction or the work itself could motivate. Instead, she offers rewards and threats as motivators: a day off, a gift certificate, a possible promotion; or, additional paperwork, a cancelled vacation, an undesirable assignment. Sometimes her threats intensify an employee's fear of failure. *If you aren't willing to work on Saturdays, you just won't make it around here.*

The manipulator's threats can take unfair advantage of the organization's policies and standards. *You can't leave for jury duty until you get your budget requests finished up.* She may lean on political influence to support her promises. *If you will take on this project, I'm sure I can get you excused from some of your other duties.* Often her personal appreciation accompanies her request. *I'll really appreciate it if you'll . . . .* Or, *I won't forget it.* She implies, of course, the opposite notion. *I will remember it if you refuse.* Or, the ultimate consequence, *You'll be fired if you don't.*

Employees often react to promised rewards or threatened punishments in two seemingly opposite ways. On the one hand, they realize they can push the manager beyond normal job standards in an effort to get more. *Will you get me extra pay if I do it?* Or, *Can I leave early if I finish up early?* On the other hand, they aim for the minimum activity required to get the benefit or to avoid the punishment. *How short can I make the report and get by with it?* Or, *How late do I have to stay to get credit for a whole day?* In any event, the manipulator's style focuses employees on the reward or threat instead of the value or quality of the task itself.

In the short-term, rewards and threats may produce desired behavior. However, in the long-term, rewards and threats establish a climate of perpetual negotiation and game playing.

In order to build revenue for his small town newspaper, publisher Lee Matthews offered $25 for each ad that his employees sold for a special holiday supplement. Most employees throughout the organization took advantage of the chance to earn extra spending money. However, Lee offered no extra incentive for ad sales in the spring supplement. Even though he again asked all employees to sell ads, no employees outside the sales department sold anything.

—L.C.D.

Eventually, the manipulator offers all the carrots that the budget or circumstances allow. However, by this time the employee views the previous rewards as rights. *I've always had a year-end bonus; I was planning to get one this year.* At that point, the manipulator may gamble on an employee's short-term memory and promise things that she cannot deliver. *We might create a new supervisor's position. I'll keep you in mind.* Or, she may personally perpetuate the rewards. *How can I get them to do what I want when I can't pay them extra? I'll have to take the top salesperson out to lunch.* When the rewards stop completely, the desired behavior usually stops as well.

Mrs. Wynn, the branch manager for a financial institution, rallied sales of travelers' checks for the month of July by developing a point system for every sale. Employee efforts went up, and sales increased 14 percent for the month. Without the incentive the following month, sales plummeted to their usual level. Subsequently, Mrs. Wynn's push to promote student loans in the fall was greeted by employees with "What are you going to pay us?"

—*L.C.D.*

The Manipulator at Home

The manipulator parent goes through the day offering rewards and threatening punishments, believing that this motivates children. *You can have your box of animal crackers if you get out of the bathtub right now.* Or, *If you are not home by eleven, you're grounded.* The manipulator dangles star charts and stickers, money and computer games. He also promises negative consequences with time-outs and grounding and withdraws privileges, such as bedtime stories and telephone time. Sometimes, he offers vague consequences for undesirable behavior. *If you can't play nicely, you can't have friends over.* Or, *If you can't turn off that TV, we're just going to have to unplug it.*

Danny's father was proud that he had provided a monetary incentive for his eight-year-old son to make the bed each morning. Within a couple of weeks, Danny was making not only his own bed but also his brother's and his parents'. When his father commented on Danny's apparent diligence, Danny replied, "I want more allowance."

— *C.C.M.*

Before long the manipulator exhausts all reasonable rewards and punishments. He grasps at whatever he thinks might work for the moment, without considering his own willingness to follow through. *If you don't sit still in the grocery cart, I'm going to take you home.* Or, *If you don't bring the car back on time, you can't have it for six months.* The child recognizes the empty threat, realizes that nothing will happen, and continues to misbehave.

Sarilyn e-mailed in desperation, asking for a way to make her six-year-old son behave. "He doesn't really have any more privileges that I can take away other than dessert and an hour of TV. So now when he misbehaves I send him to his room immediately. I start to count to ten. The understanding is that if I make it to ten and he is not in his room, he gets a spanking. He hasn't called my bluff, but the time will come."

— *C.C.M.*

When a parent models manipulation, he teaches the child how to manipulate. For example, instead of discussing how peas help you grow, he negotiates the number of peas the child must eat before she earns a bowl of ice cream. Soon, the child learns to play the game. *If I eat my peas, do I get ice cream?* Ultimately, she discovers the existence of an acceptable minimum. *How many peas do I have to eat to get ice cream?*

Preoccupied with rewards and punishments, the manipulator fails to explain the value of the behavior he seeks. Mistakenly, he believes that his motivators will create a desire within the child to repeat appropriate behavior, but the child behaves simply to get rewards or avoid punishment. The child evaluates each request in terms of its impact on her. *Do I want a smiley face sticker enough to be nice to my brother?* Or, *Do I want to stay out late tonight badly enough to risk being grounded?* When rewards and punishments lose their effect, the child has no reason to behave appropriately. The parent worries, *I just can't motivate her.*

One Sunday at church, seven-year-old Spencer seemed particularly interested in the children who wore white robes and participated in the communion service. After church his mother, Darcy, asked Spencer if he would like to become an altar server.

Spencer replied, "Do I get paid for it?"

— *C.C.M.*

Your Use of The Manipulator Style

If you have a high score in the manipulator category on either self-test, you focus on rewards or punishment to control the behavior of others. However, you actually send a different message from the one that you intend. You shift the emphasis away from appropriate behavior and toward the consequences you promise. When your employees and children fail to internalize the importance of the behavior itself, they perform at minimal levels. Your assumption that you must motivate them devalues their personal ability to motivate themselves.

Record on the following journal page words and phrases you say during the next few days that suggest the manipulator control style.

CONTROL STYLE JOURNAL: MANIPULATOR

Jot down words and phrases you say at **WORK** that suggest
the **manipulator** control style.

_____

_____

_____

_____

_____

_____

_____

_____

Jot down words and phrases you say at **HOME** that suggest
the **manipulator** control style.

_____

_____

_____

_____

_____

_____

_____

_____

THE MARTYR

Unlike the boss and the manipulator, the martyr chooses not to take control. Instead, she gives control to others, hoping that they will like her or see her as a friend. Sometimes, she abdicates control simply because she does not know what else to do. The martyr strives for harmonious relationships, avoids conflict, and protects her employees and children from unpleasant situations. A fixer by nature, the martyr goes to any length to ensure that others get what they want and do not have to account for inappropriate behavior.

The Martyr at Work

The martyr takes a passive approach to his management role. He avoids enforcing standards that will make his employees unhappy. *I couldn't tell Mia to do that. She wouldn't like it.* However, without setting limits, he feels helpless to influence performance. *Raji has always used that computer program, and he would never consider changing.* The martyr thinks avoiding managerial control will cause others to like him, but his inconsistency and lack of direction cause employees to resent his lack of leadership.

> *When Paula, a hospital supervisor, arrived for work, she noticed three nurses taking a smoke break in a no-smoking area just outside the front entrance. When Paula saw her manager, Marcella, in the hall, she complained about the smokers.*
>
> *"Why didn't you say something to them?" Marcella asked.*
>
> *Unwilling to accept that she, too, represents management, Paula replied, "If management doesn't want them to smoke there, management should tell them. I don't want them to be mad at me."*
>
> —*L.C.D.*

The martyr has difficulty holding others accountable. At times he may complete or correct their work himself in order to avoid confrontation. *Your drawings looked pretty good to me. I made a few changes and sent them on.* He notoriously evaluates all employees as satisfactory or above because he dreads discussing poor performance. In extreme cases, he may promote or transfer someone to avoid the entire issue.

From the martyr's perspective, delegating represents an imposition on employees. Typically, he compounds his personal responsibilities rather than assign them to anyone. *They're all so overworked. I don't want to bother them.*

> *I arrived early at the Superintendent's office for my eight o'clock appointment to discuss training for his small school district. His secretary informed me, "Richard is not back from the post office; the mail must be late this morning." I waited for almost an hour.*
>
> *When Richard arrived, he quickly apologized. "I'm so sorry," he said. "I just finished sorting and delivering the mail for the building. Now I am ready for our meeting."*
>
> *I asked if today's mail run was typical, and he rather hesitatingly explained. "You see, I started working for the school system when I was a high school junior. My job was to pick up, sort, and deliver the mail. I've just continued doing it. Everyone else is so busy."*
>
> —L.C.D.

The martyr excuses his employees from criticism by customers and vendors. *She didn't mean to shortchange you. She's going through a divorce right now, and she's having a hard time.* To upper management, the martyr often rationalizes poor performance. *My people are working as hard as they can.* When located away from other management support, the martyr's identification with employees intensifies. *Those people in the home office don't have any idea how hard your job is.*

The Martyr At Home

The martyr fears that setting limits will upset her child. She attempts to win her child's love by playing the role of friend or playmate. Confused about her responsibility as a parent, the martyr inappropriately asks the child's advice for what to do. *Do you want to go to bed now?* Or, *Don't you think you should give the toy back?*

The martyr gives the child virtually anything he wants because she dreads spoiling precious time with discipline. Tyler eats a hot dog every night for dinner because he never likes the family's meal. Dyan stays up until she falls asleep on the floor because she will make a scene if she is put to bed. Scotty jumps on the neighbor's couch, and the martyr ignores it to avoid upsetting him.

As the child gets older, he assumes he will continue getting his way. Any attempt to set limits becomes more difficult. Eventually, the child controls the family, and the martyr says *There's nothing I can do about it.*

> *Several years ago Blanche came to me concerned about her five-year-old son, Charles Ray. Every day when she picked him up from kindergarten at noon he insisted that she drive him to McDonald's for lunch. Charles Ray would eat nothing until the next day's trip to McDonald's. Although I advised her to stop letting Charles Ray control the situation and work with him to select one day a week for a special McDonald's meal, three months later Blanche was still making the daily drive to McDonald's.*
>
> — *C.C.M.*

The martyr has difficulty holding her child accountable for his behavior. If the child misbehaves, he is too tired, too sick, too hungry, or too young. If others try to hold him accountable, she makes excuses, blames the school, or tries to fix the situation. Because the martyr protects her child from life's difficulties, he learns to avoid activities that require effort.

Michael and Andrea shared their bed with Chelsea from the day she came home from the hospital. Three years later they called for advice. They were no longer getting a good night's sleep with Chelsea in bed with them. They were exhausted from her nightly antics, and they wished for privacy. Each time they brought up the subject of moving Chelsea into another bed, she cried and insisted that she would be unhappy sleeping alone. Michael and Andrea couldn't bear the thought of making Chelsea unhappy.

—— *C.C.M.*

In an attempt to create a perfect childhood, the martyr gives her child inappropriate privileges, expensive lessons, or excessive gifts. If she buys the wrong cartoon action figure, she exchanges it at once. Her need to make the child's life ideal may stem from her disappointment in her own childhood, her guilt about working long hours, or her effort to compensate for divorce or other circumstances.

Your Use of The Martyr Style

If you have a high score in the martyr category on either self-test, you relinquish control to your employee or child. To preserve harmony and avoid conflict, you provide little guidance and diminish the focus on appropriate behavior. You may think setting no limits endears you to others. Yet, in the long run, they disrespect your unwillingness to take a stand. Your style encourages their unrealistic belief that they will always get their way and fails to prepare them for life's inevitable give and take.

Record on the following journal page words and phrases you say during the next few days that suggest the martyr control style.

CONTROL STYLE JOURNAL: MARTYR

Jot down words and phrases you say at **WORK** that suggest
the **martyr** control style.

_____

_____

_____

_____

_____

_____

_____

_____

Jot down words and phrases you say at **HOME** that suggest
the **martyr** control style.

_____

_____

_____

_____

_____

_____

_____

_____

_____

THE MENTOR

A mentor shares wisdom about aspects of life. The mentor manager or mentor parent willingly accepts the challenge to develop responsible, self-directed people. He recognizes the ineffectiveness of attempting to control employees or children. Instead, he identifies and explains values and standards. Whether at work or at home, the mentor involves employees and children in making their own choices. Ultimately, he places responsibility for behavior in their hands.

The Mentor at Work

Unlike the boss, the mentor knows that she cannot make every decision or solve every problem. She encourages independent thinking and personal growth. *Design your route however you think it will best serve your customers.* Unlike the manipulator, the mentor trusts the initiative of each person to define and achieve personal goals. *What do you want to accomplish this quarter?* Unlike the martyr, she enforces standards and accepts unpopularity if necessary. *You need to redesign this ad using our new logo.* Although the mentor cares about her employees, she does not allow friendships to cloud her judgment about employees' progress. She has courage to end an unsuccessful employment relationship, but she preserves dignity with a caring confrontation.

The mentor translates the organization's mission and goals into daily activities. If the organization values customer service, she models good service strategies. She discusses customer service issues with her employees, evaluates their conversations with customers, and encourages them to develop their service skills.

Rhoda, the senior administrator for an e-commerce retailer, encouraged each division director to develop a strategic plan for the next fiscal year. Arnold resisted the assignment and returned to Rhoda requesting more instructions. "How do you want me to create this plan?" he asked. "And what kind of format do you have in mind for the final report?"

Rhoda's first reaction was to give him an example that outlined a successful plan. Instead, she explained, "I want you to create a realistic plan that your staff can support. Just keep your budget in mind and meet the deadline. The format is completely up to you."

Although Arnold returned several times for coaching and encouragement, his final product was unique and totally supported by the entire staff.

—————————————————————————————L.C.D.

For the mentor, employee concerns provide opportunities for discussion. Acknowledging the feelings of her employees and listening to their perspectives, she invites them to help redefine their own work standards. Unlike the boss and manipulator, she strives for consensus rather than imposing her own choices. When inevitable mistakes occur, she allows others to experience the result of their actions.

Pat was new to the insurance call center. During her first month as supervisor, she asked team members individually to describe their strengths, as well as their expectations of her. When new call center goals arrived from the home office, Pat shared them with the team and asked them to set team goals. She supported their plans and coached those who had difficulty. When the team met their first month's goals, she surprised them with a pizza celebration. After less than a year, Pat's staff nominated her for supervisor of the quarter.

—————————————————————————————L.C.D.

The mentor sees herself as a partner with her employees, building a supportive relationship based on mutual respect. She values collaboration, openly shares information, and models trust. She delights in her employees' development and recommends them for deserved promotions or positions outside her department. The mentor encourages their progress and is not threatened by their successes.

The Mentor at Home

The mentor parent recognizes the futility of trying to control his child's every behavior. Unlike the boss, he allows the child freedom to perform within established limits. *As long as you change the kitty litter weekly, the day of the week does not matter.* Unlike the manipulator, the mentor does not resort to rewards and punishments but seeks to help the child understand the importance of specific behaviors. *Going to soccer practice is important because you are part of the team.* Unlike the martyr, the mentor clearly states expectations and engages his child's cooperation. *Juan had the tricycle first. It is important to take turns. Ask him if you can have a turn when he is finished.* Above all, the mentor respects the child, values his opinions and feelings, and recognizes his unique needs.

> *Don and Clarice are extroverts who enjoy weekend dinner parties and neighborhood get-togethers. Their ten-year-old daughter Elizabeth also loves weekend social activities, although their seven-year-old son Brian is an introvert, who must have downtime to recharge. Don and Clarice were concerned about the battle required to get Brian to join the family in a constant stream of weekend events. When they recognized his need for time alone and structured part of the weekend for him to play quietly in his room, the fighting ended.*
>
> — *C.C.M.*

The mentor models important values for his family, such as honesty, kindness, or respect. His ongoing dialogue helps his child to connect values to daily expectations. If the family respects elders, the mentor translates that value into action when Grandpa comes to visit. He listens to Grandpa's stories, expresses interest in Grandpa's ideas, and includes Grandpa in family conversations. As the child matures and the mentor observes her emerging capabilities, he asks questions that cause her to think. *Grandpa really enjoyed going to your school play. Have you asked him about plays that he was in when he was a little boy?*

The mentor seeks the child's perspective about a situation. Instead of assuming that the child watched TV and left Grandpa alone, the mentor first inquires *What did you and Grandpa do after school today?* The subsequent conversation gives him an opportunity to evaluate her judgment. Eventually, the mentor can trust his daughter to make choices based on the values of their family.

> *Roberta, a single parent, valued respect. Nowhere was this more important than at the family dinner table. Roberta encouraged her two daughters, nine-year-old Stephanie and five-year-old Julianne, to practice good manners and appropriate conversational skills during dinner. However, not all evenings went smoothly! One night, Stephanie kicked Julianne under the table.*
>
> *Instead of retaliating, Julianne asked, "May I be excused?"*
>
> *When Roberta wondered why, Julianne replied, "Because if I sit here any longer I am going to have to yell at somebody."*
>
> — *C.C.M.*

Your Use of The Mentor Style

If you have a high score in the mentor category on either self-test, you strive to build respectful, collaborative relationships with your employees and children. Recognizing their capacity to make their own decisions, you encourage them to internalize the values of your organization or family as the foundation for their choices. You guide with helpful information, instruction, and advice, concentrating on direction rather than discipline. Believing in the potential of individuals, you allow them time to discover motivation and initiative within, trusting rather than controlling their behavior.

Record on the following journal page words and phrases you say during the next few days that suggest the mentor control style.

CONTROL STYLE JOURNAL: MENTOR

Jot down words and phrases you say at **WORK** that suggest
the **mentor** control style.

_____
_____
_____
_____
_____
_____
_____
_____
_____
_____

Jot down words and phrases you say at **HOME** that suggest
the **mentor** control style.

_____
_____
_____
_____
_____
_____
_____
_____
_____

THE MENTORING MODEL

The mentoring process involves four interrelated strategies. Success at one level leads to the next, and difficulty at any level allows you to revisit the previous strategy. Mentoring begins when you create a structure to explain the values and expectations of your organization or family. Building on that foundation, you coach employees and children to develop their own skills. As they become more independent, you conference to expand original expectations. Finally, as you recognize their ability to direct themselves, you let go.

Mentoring Strategies

The figure below illustrates the interrelated mentoring strategies, with the definition of each strategy appearing to the right.

Letting Go — Recognizing Responsibility and Self-Direction

Conferencing — Collaborating to Expand Expectations

Coaching — Encouraging Skill Development

Structuring — Communicating Performance Expectations

The complete mentoring model, shown on the next page, includes the skills that compose each strategy. The model is rooted in the values of the organization or family and builds to successful relationships with employees and children.

Each of the following chapters is devoted to one of the four mentoring strategies; that strategy is highlighted in the model that begins the chapter. Mastery of each strategy requires your conscious commitment and effort. Anecdotes, examples, and worksheets will guide your practice. You will look back at sections of the self-tests to gain additional insight as you develop your mentoring style.

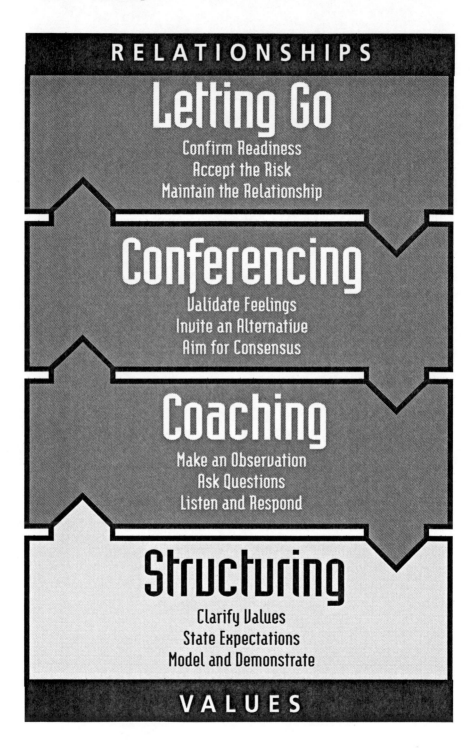

RELATIONSHIPS

Letting Go
Confirm Readiness
Accept the Risk
Maintain the Relationship

Conferencing
Validate Feelings
Invite an Alternative
Aim for Consensus

Coaching
Make an Observation
Ask Questions
Listen and Respond

Structuring
Clarify Values
State Expectations
Model and Demonstrate

VALUES

CHAPTER TWO

Structuring

Through structuring, the mentor communicates the performance expectations that determine appropriate behavior. You communicate why your organization or family holds certain values. You describe what behavior those values require. You show how to succeed by modeling and demonstrating the necessary skills. The responsibility for structuring in the mentoring relationship rests completely with the mentor; your employee or child relies on you to explain daily life in the organization or family.

YOUR STRUCTURING SCORE

Your responses to the self-tests in Chapter One determine your overall control style at work and at home. Items one through three indicate your approach to **structuring**. Transfer your answers from those items to the box on the next page. Add your scores vertically. Compare your structuring scores to the descriptions of the four structuring styles that follow.

Items Related to Structuring

SELF-TEST FOR WORK

1.	c _____	a _____	b _____	d _____
2.	b _____	c _____	a _____	d _____
3.	d _____	a _____	b _____	c _____
TOTALS	_____	_____	_____	_____
	BOSS	MANIPULATOR	MARTYR	MENTOR

SELF-TEST FOR HOME

1.	c _2_	a _4_	b _1_	d _3_
2.	b _3_	c _2_	a _1_	d _4_
3.	d _1_	a _2_	b _3_	c _4_
TOTALS	_6_	_8_	_5_	_11_
	BOSS	MANIPULATOR	MARTYR	MENTOR

HOW EACH STYLE STRUCTURES

The **boss** structures by dictating and demanding. He talks in the present tense, literally telling others what they must do. However, he fails to connect the expected behavior to a value. Without understanding a reason for the behavior, his employees and children see no need to repeat it, and he wonders why he must continue telling them what to do. The boss does not concern himself with modeling correct behavior, preferring *Do as I say, not as I do.* Boss managers give instructions and expect obedience. *Make an exception for that customer.* Or, *Clean up your workstation.* Or, *Work the late shift tomorrow.* Similarly, the boss parent says *Go comb your hair.* Or, *Feed the dog.* Or, *I said you can't have the car.*

The **manipulator** structures by pairing the request for expected behavior with a future consequence. Because the manipulator disregards underlying values, she fails to lay the foundation for long-term, responsible performance. Winning a reward or avoiding a punishment becomes the only reason for the desired behavior. Manipulator managers consistently connect behavior to contingencies. *If you'll return these calls for me, I'll let you go home early.* The manipulator parent, who motivates with treats, complains *He was clearing the table every day to get an ice cream bar. Now he is sick of them, and I have no way to get him to clear the table.*

The **martyr** avoids communicating performance expectations for fear of upsetting others. He may rely on modeling appropriate values and behavior, hoping that others will follow. Without clear guidelines, his employees and children determine their own structure. The martyr manager feels forced to accept varied performance standards. *Every teller in the bank balances at the end of the day except Lucille. She's been here forever and the customers love her, so we overlook the fact that she can't balance.* The martyr parent moans *We are exhausted, but our two-year-old just likes to stay up until eleven o'clock.*

The **mentor** structures by clearly explaining basic values that define standards of behavior within the organization or family. Her own actions consistently reflect those values. The mentor manager teaches *Completing project reports on schedule allows us to bill the client and collect payment by the end of the month.* The mentor parent takes time to explain *You need to be ready for school by seven o'clock so that I can drop you off on my way to work.*

STRUCTURING AS A STRATEGY

The mentor incorporates expectations and clear boundaries into the daily routines of the organization or family. *Make suggestions in your report for the district manager because she likes employee input.* Or, *Old school papers can be recycled, so put them in the recycle bin.* Structuring orients new employees and young children before they develop bad habits. *Anytime you leave the office, tell the secretary so that she can let your clients know how to reach you.* Or, *We wash the pots and pans last so that the greasy water does not leave a film on the dishes.*

> *When I taught at The University of Oklahoma, Colby, a freshman, sat down at my desk as my phone rang. It was a personal call. I covered the receiver and said to him politely, "Excuse me."*
>
> *"Oh, sure." He grinned and didn't move.*
>
> *Suddenly, I realized that he had no inkling of office protocol. "When you are in someone's office and they say 'Excuse me,' it means you leave so that they can have a private conversation," I explained.*
>
> *"Oh, okay." Colby ambled out into the hall.*
>
> —*L.C.D.*

The mentor manager shares his understanding of the organization's mission and relates it to daily performance expectations. If the organization values corporate growth, the mentor structures for his sales staff. *In order to develop new customers and expand our market share, each of us needs to call on five prospects a week. It is critical that we look for potential customers in new areas.*

The mentor parent talks with his preschooler about what they do as they clear the table. *When we put the dishes in the dishwasher right after breakfast, then the kitchen is clean and we can use the table for playdough.* This parent identifies orderliness as an important value and clearing dishes as an expectation. Many parents share this belief and also model this behavior; however, the mentor parent explains the reason as he demonstrates.

When the mentor structures, he ties the expected behavior (calling on five new prospects a week or putting dishes in the dishwasher) to the value from which it originates (corporate growth or orderliness). The employee or preschooler begins to build internal reasons for repeating this behavior. As an employee or child develops appropriate habits and becomes more experienced, her limits expand to allow more freedom and responsibility.

When employees and children do not understand underlying values, they may fail to comply. Without structure, the salesperson might interpret *You need to sell more* to mean *Your existing customers need to buy more.* To structure properly, her manager would explain *We always want to expand our customer base, so it is important for you to sell to new customers.* If on a busy day the parent says, *Oh, just push the dirty dishes aside and play with your playdough,* the inconsistency sends a mixed message.

Three-year-old Katie liked to play in her backyard with Gregory, the two-year-old who lived next door. He was afraid to play there because of Katie's dog and wanted Katie's mom to stay in the backyard. One day Katie's mom had to work in the garage and knew that Gregory would not play in the backyard without her. Unfortunately, she did not explain today's difference to the children. All she said was "You have to play alone in the front yard today." Katie screamed, bit her mom on the arm, and Gregory went home.

—— *C.C.M.*

Some managers and parents fail to structure, believing *They should already know this.* Or, *I shouldn't have to tell them.* Or, *They should know better.* These assumptions seem reasonable. However, if managers and parents say nothing or depend only on modeling, others may not understand it, appreciate it, relate to it, or internalize it. This allows the employee or child to insist *Nobody told me!*

Mr. Skeil hired two high school students to run his sandwich shop after school. They seemed friendly during the interview, and he thought they would work well with customers. Without further instruction, Ramona and Adele let their classmates stop by to visit and come behind the counter to chat, while ignoring adult customers. Mr. Skeil, who rarely came by the shop during the afternoon, couldn't understand why afternoon sales continued to drop.

—*L.C.D.*

Employees bring to the workplace diverse personality traits, generational beliefs, and life experiences. They arrive with a variety of perceptions, including distinct views of customer service, telephone etiquette, and professional dress. Employees have no reason to broaden their perceptions without a clear description of the precise behavior that the organization expects.

Parents may believe that modeling without explanation or telling a child once should cause the child always to put the bag of potato chips away or park the car in the garage. Yet, effective structuring requires repetition, consistency, and patience. Structuring works best in a calm moment because negative emotions interfere with learning. Mentor managers and mentor parents recognize the need to cool down before initiating a structuring conversation.

Cleaning the kitchen after dinner, John told his eight-year-old daughter, "Tiana, put away the chicken." Using plastic wrap, she covered the entire baking pan containing only two leftover pieces. John noticed Tiana trying to fit the large pan in the refrigerator. "Why on earth did you leave it in that big dish?"

Later, John and his wife, Audrey, realized that Tiana had never been involved in putting food away. The next night after dinner, John and Tiana were in the kitchen again. From the adjoining room, Audrey heard John beginning, "Now, Tiana, when you load the dishwasher, the first thing you do is . . . ."

— *C.C.M.*

Structuring at Work

Every organization expects certain behaviors and outcomes, formally written or mutually understood. When the mentor manager explains procedures, she relates the organization's values to daily expectations. *We double-check all our computations because our firm has a reputation for accuracy.* Or, *Patient education is important to us, so explain any prescription side effects before patients leave the pharmacy.*

When employees receive clear directions and specific expectations, they work with confidence. *Our restaurant's customers must be satisfied with their meals, so offer to take back any unsatisfactory item.* A new employee with experience in another organization needs to know what is different from the former workplace. Unclear direction at work costs time and money, contributes to unfocused effort, and leads to employee dissatisfaction.

> *Amy, the president of a corporation that owns juvenile detention centers, oriented new employees to a basic value. "When you make decisions," she explained, "remember that caring for children is our only focus here. Always put children first."*
>
> *When the director of Human Resources considered a proposal to lower health care costs by eliminating benefits for the children, her decision was easy: lower costs some other way.*
>
> —*L.C.D.*

Assigning a new task or changing a procedure also requires structuring. The mentor must clarify how the new task contributes to the big picture. *The new system automatically calculates sales tax, so from now on enter the sale price only.* Or, *Our teachers need to keep written observations of each student because the new report cards will include anecdotal records.*

Structuring at Home

Children need to understand reasons for parental instructions. Without knowing the underlying value, they often perceive that parents simply order them around. Children may assert their autonomy or growing independence by refusing to comply, especially if they do not see their parents modeling the same behavior. The child may say *I'm not making my bed anymore. You never make yours!* When a situation differs from what children have come to expect, they need to understand how the structure changed. The parent needs to explain *Your soccer game is an hour earlier today, so take your uniform to school because you won't have time to come home to change.*

> *Compton and Juanita described the aggressive behavior of Parker, their five-year-old son, "Parker head-butts Compton in the crotch, throws his little sister to the ground, and jumps on Juanita anytime she sits down. Parker doesn't seem angry. We think he just likes to wrestle. We have wrestled with him since he was little. Now we are wondering if we have modeled inappropriate ways to play."*
>
> *I suggested that Compton and Juanita sit down with Parker and respectfully say, "You know, Parker, we realize that we made a mistake when we encouraged you to wrestle with us. But we are going to stop wrestling with you now because it is teaching you that jumping on people is okay. Let's work together to find ways to play that don't hurt people."*
>
> — *C.C.M.*

When introduced to family routines at a young age, children likely will make these routines a part of their own lives. Two-year-olds have limited prior experience and eagerly respond to a parent who demonstrates washing hands. But try explaining this habit to a thirteen-year-old!

Parents must understand the developmental level of the child and realize that it takes time for children to internalize values. A young child may take a purple crayon from a neighbor or a pack of gum from the store simply because she wants it. She does not yet understand how taking something that does not belong to her relates to the value of honesty. Rather than shaming her, take advantage of the opportunity to explain your values and show her what to do. *We must always pay for things before we take them from the store. We need to go back to the store so that you can return the gum and explain that you took it without paying for it.*

Understanding developmental levels also helps mentor parents to teach only relevant aspects of the daily routine. The preschooler wants to know about daily health habits and social activities. *After you eat breakfast, brush your teeth so that you are all ready for the day.* Or, *If you want to swing, you need to ask for a turn.* When the child goes to school, the parent takes advantage of teachable moments to talk about values and expectations for completing homework, going places with other children, and conforming to current fads in music and dress. By the time children enter adolescence, clear expectations encompass driving, alcohol, and drugs.

STRUCTURING SKILLS

The structuring strategy focuses on daily performance expectations. As a mentor, you establish structure for your employee or child when you practice the following three skills.

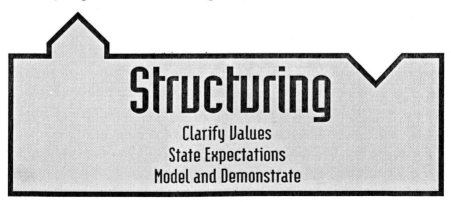

Structuring
Clarify Values
State Expectations
Model and Demonstrate

Structuring Skill: Clarify Values

Clearly stated values answer the ultimate **why** about behavior. They explain the reason for appropriate choices within your organization or family. In organizations, common beliefs describe culture. *We value quality, so quality is our most important product.* For families, values help define identity. *We Johnsons value community service, so our boys have always been Eagle Scouts.* Your organization or family shares common beliefs, even if unstated. However, when organizations and families express their values, reasons for expected behavior become easier to understand.

> *Kevin could tell I was not pleased when I picked up my order at the copy shop. He asked me how it looked, and I expressed my dissatisfaction. The text was crooked on each page. To my amazement, he dropped the entire 500 pages in the recycle bin and said, "Done wrong, done over. We'll have a new set in ten minutes–no charge!"*
>
> *Knowing he was new to the shop, I asked if he had the authority to reprint such a large order.*
>
> *"Sure," explained Kevin. "If an order is done wrong, it must be done over. Done wrong, done over. Any one of us has the authority to make that decision."*
>
> —*L.C.D.*

Members of organizations and families appreciate behaviors that represent their shared values. When an organization believes in customer service, its employees will consider it worthwhile to answer the phone by the third ring, stop everything to wait on a customer, and accept any returned items without questions. When a family values health, its members consider it worthwhile to sleep regular hours, exercise routinely, and eat nutritious food.

Most managers and parents see inappropriate behavior and simply say *Don't do that!* However, your role continually requires you to explain reasons for behavior. Sometimes, living the values proves easier than explaining them. You may not have given much thought to the values that underlie your organization's preference for sharing cleanup duties in the break room or your family's preference for an uncluttered living room. You simply know these expectations. Even so, you must clarify the values of your organization or family before you can articulate them to others. The following process may help you determine what to say. Ask yourself what about the behavior seems inappropriate. Then describe what appropriate behavior should look like. Finally, ask yourself why, which will help you identify the underlying value.

Clarifying Values

1. **What specific behavior seems inappropriate?**

2. **What should appropriate behavior look like?**

3. **Why? What is the underlying value?**

---

1. What specific behavior seems inappropriate?

The process of clarifying values begins with observing specific behavior that seems unacceptable. *Melanie does not attend required meetings.* Or, *Clay calls his sister names when they disagree.* Your observation allows you to describe the inappropriate behavior. Avoid referring to conduct in vague terms *Melanie has a bad attitude.* Or, *Clay is always so mean to his sister.* Phrases such as *bad attitude* or *always so mean* do not explicitly define unacceptable behavior. Further, productive discussion about the behavior cannot take place without a definite point of reference.

> *Marcia was overwhelmed with the out-of-control behavior of her four-year-old son, Duncan. I noticed, however, that she only talked about her reactions and did not describe what Duncan said or did that was inappropriate.*
>
> *"He will never see the inside of a grocery store until he is six. I am tired of being stared at by other shoppers. I feel like a freak or someone with three eyes. We don't do malls or restaurants. McDonald's is a big deal. Big holiday dinners at Grandma's are avoided at all costs; we are not above feigning illness."*
>
> — *C.C.M.*

2. What should appropriate behavior look like?

Once you identify specific inappropriate conduct, you can more easily characterize appropriate behavior. When Melanie does not attend your required meeting, her absence causes you to realize *Melanie must attend required meetings.* When Clay calls his sister names, you think *Anytime Clay disagrees with his sister, he needs to tell her exactly what is bothering him.*

Sometimes, you identify appropriate behavior as a result of an emotional reaction rather than through a careful thought process. You see an employee come to work late and immediately blow up, *Ramiro, you were supposed to be here at eight!* When you struggle to get your toddler in her car seat, your frustration may erupt in *Get in your car seat!* These experiences hit an emotional hot button for you, nevertheless your realization defines appropriate behavior.

3. Why? What is the underlying value?

Identifying correct behavior logically leads you to question *why?* Why do those in your organization or family believe in the appropriateness of that particular conduct? Your position that employees must attend required meetings may come from your commitment to cooperation. The expectation that employees should arrive on time may come from the importance of timeliness. As a family, your belief in straightforward communication stems from your value of respecting others. Your insistence that toddlers should ride in car seats originates in your concern for safety.

James and his teenage son Daniel were in church one Sunday morning. Daniel slouched in the pew and frequently talked loudly enough for others to hear. Angrily, James gestured and glared at Daniel to no avail.

When they returned home, James realized that he needed to cool down before he talked to Daniel about his behavior. As he reflected on the situation, James realized that his strong feelings were due to his own observations and judgments about other teenagers in church. When he was able to explain the importance of respectful behavior in church, he went to Daniel.

James calmly shared, "Do you know what I think when I see teenagers in church who are not respectful?" Sharing his values without blaming allowed James to have an open discussion with his son. The next Sunday Daniel's respectful church behavior came as a pleasant surprise.

— *C.C.M.*

Values define common abstract beliefs that bring structure to the organization or family. In early childhood, **health, safety,** and **respect** generally govern children's behavior. Expectations include *wash your hands before you eat, look and listen before you cross the street,* and *take turns playing with toys.* As children grow, families expand their structure with additional values such as **responsibility, relationships, honesty and integrity, teamwork, family and cultural heritage,** and **service.** Organizations add their own values, which may include **quality and quantity of work, timeliness, innovation,** and **customer service.** These may generate expectations that employees will *aim for continuous quality, start meetings on time, continually improve processes,* and *greet each customer.*

More effectively taught and reinforced at home, some values build the foundation for relationships throughout life, including kindness, confidentiality, courage, tact, courtesy, and tolerance. Still others, such as trustworthiness, enthusiasm, assertiveness, friendliness, loyalty, reliability, determination, and excellence can directly contribute to success in the workplace. Teaching children to relate their behavior to positive values gives them both an interpersonal and organizational advantage. If parents fail to address these issues, the organization must.

As you determine the values of your organization or family, you will discover consistency with most of your personal beliefs or preferences. *I value flexibility and so does my organization because they allow me to job share.* Or, *I believe in family relationships and want to encourage my children to know their cousins.* However, your personal notions may go beyond what the organization or family expects of every member. Insisting that employees or children meet your personal values often results in struggles for control. Your personal value of accuracy might require department store cashiers to balance to the penny, yet the store's value of expediency may allow them to dismiss any outage under a dollar. Insisting that your seventh grader wear his cap frontward responds to your personal value of image rather than your family's value of clean clothing.

> As the new manager of the medical office, Alice learned about "Pig Out Fridays": traditional potluck lunches to which nurses and clerks contributed favorite foods. Immediately, Alice ended the tradition by saying, "I'm offended that these ladies would refer to themselves as 'pigs.'"
>
> ———*L.C.D.*

Frequently, you will discover that your organization or family upholds conflicting values. Organizations that value both accuracy and timeliness sometimes face a dilemma between *accurate-but-late* reports or *ballpark-but-on-time* reports. The family that values both honesty and respect for property is in a quandary when their eight-year-old admits that he broke the living room lamp.

Maeko and Neil were concerned that their two school-age boys were not doing enough around the house. They described what David and Hiroshi already do consistently:

- *David helps Neil put out the garbage on Wednesday nights.*

- *Both David and Hiroshi help set the table and empty the dishwasher if asked, although Hiroshi doesn't like to empty the silverware.*

- *Both David and Hiroshi consistently clear their places after meals.*

When asked what values underlie their desire for the boys to help more, Maeko and Neil said that the boys should realize that family members help around the house. However, they acknowledged that they also value completing homework, having fun after school, getting a good night's sleep, and being involved in school activities. Maeko and Neil realized that David and Hiroshi were already meeting many of their family's values.

— C.C.M.

Clarifying values requires you to distinguish between what you truly value and what you say you value.

As a manager, you might ask a team to revise a policy, then veto their solution. You may say you value teamwork and participation, when you truly value maintaining the status quo.

As a parent, you may claim to value family relationships and spending time at home, yet fill your evenings with PTA board meetings, church choir practice, and hospital guild meetings. Your true operative value is community involvement.

Organizations and families sometimes misinterpret values, even among themselves.

Thomas, the CEO of a large manufacturing plant, stressed to me that his organization "values dropping everything in order to solve a problem immediately." Several weeks later at two o'clock on a Friday afternoon, Thomas called me to request facilitation of a senior management team conflict. Remembering our initial discussion and anticipating a long meeting, I mentally changed dinner plans and replied, "I can be there in thirty minutes."

"Oh, no, not today," Thomas responded. "We all have tee times at four o'clock! We were thinking of one day next week."

————————————————————————L.C.D.

When you clarify values, you ask why your organization or family appreciates certain behaviors. This requires candid, unhurried discussion. At work, it may involve a conversation with your immediate manager, or it may include several levels of management. At home, parents must make time to share with each other the values behind their expectations. Sometimes, a parent's own child-hood experiences shape values, and you must explore those with respect. When you can clearly explain the reasons for expected behavior to your employees and children, you can move beyond a focus on control.

Examples of the value-clarification process follow, along with a worksheet for your practice.

CLARIFYING VALUES AT WORK - EXAMPLES

EXAMPLE #1

1. **What specific behavior seems inappropriate?**
   Ralph didn't return tools to the shed.

2. **What should appropriate behavior look like?**
   He must always return tools to the shed when he is through with them.

3. **Why? What is the underlying value?**
   We believe in cooperation by making sure unused tools are available for others.

EXAMPLE #2

1. **What specific behavior seems inappropriate?**
   Elaine told a customer who asked for a rush order that we could not deliver on time.

2. **What should appropriate behavior look like?**
   For faster delivery, she needs to fax a rush order directly to the warehouse.

3. **Why? What is the underlying value?**
   We believe in providing the fastest possible service.

CLARIFYING VALUES AT HOME - EXAMPLES

EXAMPLE #1

1. **What specific behavior seems inappropriate?**
   My ten-year-old refuses to eat his broccoli.

2. **What should appropriate behavior look like?**
   He needs to eat vegetables.

3. **Why? What is the underlying value?**
   We believe good nutrition contributes to good health.

EXAMPLE #2

1. **What specific behavior seems inappropriate?**
   My teenager takes the car at night, and I don't know where she is.

2. **What should appropriate behavior look like?**
   When she takes the car, she needs to let me know where she is going.

3. **Why? What is the underlying value?**
   We value her safety and need to know where she might be in case there is a problem.

CLARIFYING VALUES AT WORK - PRACTICE

PRACTICE #1

1. What specific behavior seems inappropriate?

   _____

   _____

   _____

2. What should appropriate behavior look like?

   _____

   _____

   _____

3. Why? What is the underlying value?

   _____

   _____

   _____

PRACTICE #2

1. What specific behavior seems inappropriate?

   _____

   _____

   _____

2. What should appropriate behavior look like?

   _____

   _____

   _____

3. Why? What is the underlying value?

   _____

   _____

   _____

CLARIFYING VALUES AT HOME - PRACTICE

PRACTICE #1

1. What specific behavior seems inappropriate?

    _____
    _____
    _____

2. What should appropriate behavior look like?

    _____
    _____
    _____

3. Why? What is the underlying value?

    _____
    _____
    _____

PRACTICE #2

1. What specific behavior seems inappropriate?

    _____
    _____
    _____

2. What should appropriate behavior look like?

    _____
    _____
    _____

3. Why? What is the underlying value?

    _____
    _____
    _____

Structuring Skill: State Expectations

Statements of expectation identify **what** the employee or child must do. They derive from the values of your organization or family and define appropriate behavior. *We like innovative ideas around here, so feel free to make suggestions anytime you see something we could change.* Or, *Family relationships are important, so we all need to be home on Sunday when Grandmother comes to visit.* These statements clearly explain the underlying values for limits and standards, not only in this instance, but also in the future.

New situations demand that you pair the value statement with the expected behavior. However, to an experienced employee or child, you may simply imply the value. The trained employee will respond to *Look at this and tell me what you think* with the understanding that the organization welcomes innovative ideas. As the child grows, she remembers that *We all need to be home on Sunday when Grandmother comes to visit* implies that family relationships have worth, and she should arrange her schedule accordingly. Whether you state or imply your value, it always serves as the foundation for expected behavior.

When you state expectations, rely on the following key principles.

Stating Expectations

1. Expectations are specific.

2. Expectations are positive.

3. Expectations are realistic.

4. Expectations are respectful.

5. Expectations are expressed.

1. Expectations are specific.

Handle this! and *Hurry up!* are expressions that give the vague impression that something needs to happen without a clear notion of what or why. Instead, offer both a value and specific information about a single behavior. *We want to make this customer happy. Please give her a call and offer to replace or repair the defective carpet.* Or, *We want to be on time for Sunday School, so you need to get your jacket on and be ready to get in the car at nine-thirty.*

> *Pamela was concerned about two-year-old Jami's safety. Every time they left their house to get in the car, Jami raced down the sidewalk as fast as she could. Pamela and I discussed talking with Jami about safety, as well as letting Jami carry her own diaper bag in order to slow her down.*
>
> *Two weeks later Pamela laughingly told me that we had misinterpreted Jami's dashing down the sidewalk. "Yesterday when I told Jami we were going to run errands, she asked, 'Okay, Mom, are we really going to run this time, or are we going to take the car?'"*
>
> — *C.C.M.*

2. Expectations are positive.

Expectations suggest what to do rather than what not to do. *Always write information in personnel files legibly* explains more clearly how to keep good records than *Don't be sloppy when you write in personnel files.* Saying *Pet the cat gently from head to tail* teaches more about respect for family animals than *Don't pull the cat's tail.* People tend to resent *Don't do this* and *Don't do that.* In a negative environment, adults tend to shut down or become argumentative. Children begin to adopt this way of speaking and soon tell their parents *Don't tell me what to do.*

> *The dispatcher at the moving company was stating positive expectations to his estimator. "Now, Jesse, when you go out to estimate the*

moving costs, always look for a piano or a pool table, and be sure to go in the attic and the basement." However, he couldn't resist finishing with *"But don't you dare track mud on that lady's carpet or stink up her house with your smelly cigar!"*

—*L.C.D.*

3. Expectations are realistic.

Often you must adjust your expectations to fit specific circumstances. You may expect timely information from your delivery drivers when you give them handheld computers. However, unless you provide computer training, they will not know how to input the data and will resent your unrealistic expectation. You may value neatness and expect your preschooler to keep her white shoes clean. Yet, if you take her to the park for the afternoon, change your expectation or change her shoes!

4. Expectations are respectful.

Give information in a caring, supportive, and nonthreatening manner. *You'd better not take any more breaks until you finish all the data entry* threatens the employee and gives no information regarding how to make choices about future projects. *Plan your work in order to enter all relevant data by each deadline* helps the employee understand both the value of planning and the basis for her own future decisions about breaks.

I can't believe you always spill the dog food. You just won't be able to feed the dog if you can't quit that. Such statements demean young children. The child feels fearful and overwhelmed when you negatively generalize one situation to all future events. In order to generalize positively about household cleanliness, say *The dog food spilled, here's the broom. Anytime that happens again, just get the broom to clean it up.*

5. Expectations are expressed.

Sometimes, managers and parents see no reason to state expectations. They may assume others know what they mean or can interpret expectations from looks or gestures and may feel frustrated when others cannot read their minds.

> *Jake, the shift supervisor in the manufacturing plant, complained that his employees took too much time coming back from breaks. I asked him how he let them know that this was unacceptable. He explained, "When they come back, I just glare at the clock and then I glare at them."*
>
> *"And what does that teach them?" I prompted.*
>
> *Uncomfortably, Jake reflected, "That they can come back late."*
>
> —*L.C.D.*

In some instances, nonverbal behavior does support expectations. However, you cannot rely on actions alone. First, you must describe appropriate behavior clearly and directly. If in doubt about what to say, just state your value. *Customers come first.* Or, *I don't like hitting.* Sometimes, that will do. Reminding yourself of the **why** helps you express **what** you expect.

> *Six-year-old Alyson had trouble going to sleep in her own bed. Each evening after her parents tucked her in, she repeatedly tried to get in bed with them. Her mom and dad talked with her about their value of self-reliance and the expected bedtime behavior. When she would come out of her room, they would repeat, "Everyone sleeps in their own beds. We sleep in our bed, and you sleep in your bed."*
>
> *After numerous weary nights, Alyson's parents knew that she understood the value and the expectation. Further, they believed that talking just prolonged bedtime. They began to take her by the hand and walk*

her back to her bed without saying anything. In just a few nights, Alyson was staying in bed after being tucked in at bedtime.

———————————————————————————— *C.C.M.*

The following examples and worksheets illustrate how to verbalize expectations effectively. Select those that feel comfortable to you and that suit your specific situation. Have patience with yourself and others as you practice. You may feel awkward or believe you continually repeat expectations. Yet, employees and children need time to internalize values, process information, and meet behavioral expectations.

STATING EXPECTATIONS - EXAMPLES

From now on you need to...

...use spell-check on a letter before you give it to me to sign.

...be sure the dog has gone to the bathroom before you bring him inside.

When you _____ , then you _____ .

...use the video recorder...recharge the battery.

...finish riding your bike...put it away in the garage.

Anytime that happens again...

...call the officer on duty.

...just get a sponge to clean it up.

Always...

...lock that side door when you leave.

...throw dirty towels down the laundry chute.

(State the limit.) You may _____ or _____.

The order must go out today. You may send it in the morning or afternoon mail.

Running is for outside. You may go in the backyard, or we can go to the park after lunch.

*I know/see _____ . After you _____ , then you _____ .

I know that project is important to you. After you complete the monthly report, then you will have time to work on your project.

I see you want to go outside to play in the snow. After you put on your coat and boots, then you will be ready to go.

*The word "after" implies structure and denotes a mentoring strategy. Changing this word to "if" implies a contingency and denotes a manipulative strategy.

STATING EXPECTATIONS - PRACTICE

Identify several issues for which you would like to be able to state clearer expectations:

1.

_____

_____

_____

_____

_____

_____

2.

_____

_____

_____

_____

_____

3.

_____

_____

_____

_____

_____

_____

Now try the starters on the following page for restating these issues. Each issue will work better with some starters than others.

STATING EXPECTATIONS - PRACTICE

From now on you need to...

    Manager: _____

    Parent: _____

When you _____ , then you _____ .

    Manager: _____

    Parent: _____

Anytime that happens again...

    Manager: _____

    Parent: _____

Always...

    Manager: _____

    Parent: _____

(State the limit.) You may _____ or _____ .

    Manager: _____

    Parent: _____

*I know/see _____ . After you _____ , then you _____ .

    Manager: _____

    Parent: _____

*The word "after" implies structure and denotes a mentoring strategy. Changing this word to "if" implies a contingency and denotes a manipulative strategy.

Structuring Skill: Model and Demonstrate

You show others how to meet expectations when you model and demonstrate. These two techniques differ in several distinct ways, even though they achieve the same purpose.

Modeling relates to your own behavior and cannot be learned. You simply live your life, while others continually watch your actions and infer your values and expectations. Although modeling happens unintentionally, its effectiveness increases with your conscious attention.

Demonstrating intentionally focuses on the behavior of others through instruction, conversation, and participation. An effective demonstration always involves planning what others need to learn, talking about correct procedures, and involving the learner in performance. Although demonstrating is a critical skill to learn, modeling is the more important life skill to develop.

Modeling

How you act reflects your values and serves as a model of your expectations. Your actions always speak louder than your words. You may know the computer system well enough to take a shortcut. However, your new employee observes your technique and devalues the worth of the full procedure. You may receive a traffic ticket after picking up the children at school and prefer to discuss it with your spouse in a quiet moment after dinner. However, what message do your children receive about the value of honesty when you ask them not to say anything about the ticket?

Madelyn is the mother of two daughters, five-year-old Sarah and baby Caitlyn. Because she was busy with the new baby, Madelyn hired a house cleaning service to come once a week. Exhausted, she looked forward to the nights when she could say, "The cleaning service comes in the morning. I'm just going to bed and leave the house a mess."

One day it was time to take Sarah to a friend's house. Madelyn reminded her that she needed to pick up her toys first. With hands on her hips, Sarah replied, "Just let the 'cleaner lady' do it!"

— *C.C.M.*

Managers often rely on modeling alone. *Isn't it enough that they see me shut down my computer before I leave for the day?* Or, *I double-check my work for errors. Don't they see that?* Even if an employee observes your actions, you cannot assume that he will consciously choose to emulate you. If he identifies with you, he may observe closely in order to follow in your footsteps. But if he differs from you in age, gender, socioeconomic level, ethnicity, or culture, he may not identify with you strongly enough to picture himself behaving like you.

At an oil refinery on a windy hill, blowing trash really bothered Frank, the new refinery manager. Without making an issue of it, he began picking up the trash in his path as he walked between buildings. Frank found an empty barrel, moved it to a central spot and began throwing his trash collection in it.

Others began picking up trash and after a few months someone painted the barrel with the refinery colors. When a survey of the employees a year later asked how they would describe their particular refinery, 87% responded "attractive."

—*L.C.D.*

Your credibility relies on your consistency because others quickly realize when your actions contradict what you say. Because young children strive to imitate you, they openly accept the values and expectations that you model. However, as children grow older, they more easily observe character flaws in their parents. Your teenager immediately recognizes that your telephone calls go beyond his thirty-minute limit.

Inconsistency in your own behavior stems from one of two reasons: impulsive choices or conflicting values. The following guidelines will help you become aware of these pitfalls and ensure consistency between your values and your personal behavior.

Modeling Values and Expectations

1. **If you value it and expect others to do it, you must do it yourself.**

2. **Exceptions should be legitimate and explained to others.**

---

1. If you value it and expect others to do it, you must do it yourself.

When you impulsively choose to do or say what feels good at the moment, you ignore your mentoring role. You violate stated values, giving others implied permission to do the same. For example, your organization encourages returning phone calls on the same day. Even so, on one Friday when you want to leave early, you put off returning calls until the following Monday. Your employees may resent this inconsistency and postpone returning their calls. You tell your children that they should treat others with respect. However, the children recognize your inconsistency when you spend the evening arguing with the neighbor over the back fence. Next week their excuse for fighting on the school playground may become *You did it!*

2. Exceptions should be legitimate and explained to others.

Inconsistency between your words and deeds may also involve a legitimate choice between two conflicting values. When your conduct cannot serve as an immediate model for your employee or child, explain the reason for the exception. *I do insist on starting meetings promptly. However, taking five minutes to answer an employee's serious question justifies starting late.* Or, *I want to go to your ball game, but Grandmother's doctor could only see her at four o'clock. She depends on me to take her. I'll get to the game as soon as I can.*

Consciously modeling your values in the presence of others every day requires tremendous effort. Still, you cannot take yourself too seriously. Use humor to allow employees and children opportunity for release. Laugh at a harmless joke on yourself, participate in a crazy clothes day, or lead a funny skit before a training session.

> *Julie had tried to help her employees cope with the stress of the last few weeks. The credit union was short-handed because of summer vacations, and the pace was harried. By Friday afternoon, everyone had had it!*
>
> *When the office closed, Julie moved the lobby furniture out of the way and called the employees. When they arrived, she gave each a can of Silly String and, armed with her own can, led the fight. Ten minutes and many laughs later, they cleaned up the mess together and headed for home–less stressed and ready for the weekend.*
>
> —*L.C.D.*

With children, preserve the joy in each day and share pleasure in the little things in the child's life: the yellow dandelion flower, the sight of a bird in the tree, and peanut butter and jelly sandwiches on the back porch. Above all, maintain and model a sense of humor!

> *Francine took her preschool daughter, Jane Ann, with her on all the morning errands–in and out of the car at the cleaners, pharmacy, grocery store, and video store. After lunch Francine realized that she had forgotten an important ingredient for the evening meal and had to go back to the grocery store.*

Francine realized that three-year-old Jane Ann would probably resist her verbal instruction to get back in the car. She said, "We need one more thing from the store. Let's see if we can hop like bunnies to the door." Instead of entering a battle of wills with Jane Ann, Francine modeled a fun way to get to the car. Jane Ann agreeably joined her.

——————————————————————————————————— *C.C.M.*

Use the following examples and worksheet to examine your own behavior.

MODELING VALUES AND EXPECTATIONS

EXAMPLE #1

If you value it and expect others to do it, you must do it yourself.

MANAGER: *Devoting time in the office to work-related activities is important, so we all must limit personal phone calls. I will call my daughter during my lunch break.*

PARENT: *Our family likes an uncluttered kitchen. Snack dishes go in the dishwasher instead of on the counter. I need to put mine in the dishwasher as soon as I finish eating.*

EXAMPLE #2

Exceptions should be legitimate and explained to others.

MANAGER: *We don't usually close our doors around here, but I am working on the annual budget and must have no interruptions until I am finished.*

PARENT: *This trip to San Francisco is for Mom and Dad to have a weekend together. You can go with us on a family vacation.*

MODELING VALUES AND EXPECTATIONS

PRACTICE #1

If you value it and expect others to do it, you must do it yourself.

MANAGER: _____
_____
_____
_____
_____

PARENT: _____
_____
_____
_____
_____

PRACTICE #2

Exceptions should be legitimate and explained to others.

MANAGER: _____
_____
_____
_____
_____

PARENT: _____
_____
_____
_____

Demonstrating

When you demonstrate, you teach others specifically **how** to perform. As a mentor, you assess the steps and techniques others need to know, anticipate teachable moments, and encourage hands-on practice.

At work, your demonstrations support rather than replace formal training programs. For frontline supervisors, much of the day involves training about technical procedures, such as how to create a spreadsheet or how to run a delivery route. At other levels of management, demonstrations involve teaching more interpersonal or administrative skills, such as how to lead a meeting or prepare a budget. Time pressure often leads managers to shortcut the process by quickly showing *Here's what you have to do* and then walking away. However, employees often falter without personal involvement and participation.

> *In management seminars, I often use a popular training video that depicts a coworker showing a payroll computer program to a computer novice. He works through every step of the program without allowing any employee involvement. As viewers watch the trainee's eyes glaze over, they always laugh sympathetically, anticipating the predicament when the trainer leaves.*
>
> —*L.C.D.*

Demonstrating works well with children. By nature they learn best through hands-on experience, and their curiosity makes them eager to participate. They want you to notice their readiness to learn new tasks, such as loading film in the camera or power-washing the deck. Sometimes, young children enjoy having their parents take photos of them at each step of the process. Posting their photos sequentially on a chart helps them remember all the steps without your verbal reminders. Photos of your child cleaning each area of his room or following the steps in his bedtime routine will encourage self-direction.

For children, the more you involve their five senses in the demonstration, the more lasting the learning. Your child will remember the experience of making a coconut cake if you let him smell the vanilla extract and taste the coconut. Children learn best from concrete experiences with real objects. If you want to teach your child how to wash the dog, the learning simply falls short if you try demonstrating with a stuffed animal!

> *On a particularly difficult day with four-year-old Norman and two-year-old Anna, Debbie sighed, "We just need to start over! Let's shut the blinds and pretend it's night." She shut the blinds and went back to bed.*
>
> *Norman and Anna quizzically watched their mother, looked at each other, and went back into their rooms also. Shortly, Debbie came back out, pleased that she had stumbled on a way to demonstrate how to de-escalate tension.*
>
> *From then on when things got tense, Debbie encouraged a "start over." Together, the three closed all the blinds and went back in their rooms, soon to emerge ready to begin the day again.*
>
> — *C.C.M.*

As you demonstrate, distinguish your personal preferences from value-based behaviors. Let the employee create his own approach through his experience. He may work best with suppliers on the phone instead of in person like you do. As long as he complies with the organization's value *(we value close partnership with our vendors)* and meets expectations for performance *(keep vendors informed of our future needs),* let him use his personal strengths to meet your objectives. With children, too, distinguish your personal habits from your child's emerging preferences. Your two-year-old, for example, might prefer foods not to touch each other on the plate and choose to eat all of one food before moving on to the next. As long as she eats, let her do it her way.

At work and at home, rely on the following guide to demonstrate your expectations: **teach, talk,** and **two-way.**

Demonstrating Expectations

1. Teach to the learner's skill level.

2. Talk about your expectations as you show the steps.

3. Two-way participation keeps the learner involved.

1. Teach to the learner's skill level.

As you evaluate readiness, remember that employees or children may claim understanding of a process without having actual skill or experience. Their casual observations may lead to wrong conclusions. An employee may believe *Since I've seen Mary cut and paste on that computer program a hundred times, I'm sure I can figure it out.* Or, your teenager may think *Dad just pulls the car out of the garage and lets the old oil out. How hard can it be to change the oil?* Demonstrate at the individual's actual rather than self-perceived skill level.

> *Essien let seven-year-old Latoya sit on his lap as he drove his truck around the neighborhood. He showed her how to shift and turn the steering wheel, although Essien worked the accelerator and brake.*
>
> *One day Latoya waited in the truck, while Essien returned a tool to a neighbor. The next thing Essien knew there was a loud crash and the house shook. Latoya had used her driving skills to run the truck into the neighbor's house!*
>
> — *C.C.M.*

Begin by identifying the skills that the employee or child needs to know. Focus on a specific expectation, such as setting up the conference room for a training session or mowing the lawn. To avoid demeaning or overwhelming, consider what the person already knows. Observe or ask questions to assess skill, experience, and readiness. *Since Riley's been here, she's attended three training sessions. She should be ready to learn how to set up the room for the next one. Or, Chris, you've been asking questions about mowing the lawn. Would you like to learn how to do it yourself?*

2. Talk about your expectations as you show the steps.

Always begin your demonstration with familiar information to build rapport and self-confidence. *The folding tables we use for training sessions are in the cabinet at the back of the training room. Or, You've probably wondered why I always put the mower on the concrete driveway to check the gas level.*

Move slowly to unfamiliar information, remembering to state your expectation clearly. *From now on, set up the room to accommodate the number of participants listed on the set-up sheet. This floor plan details various ways you can arrange the room. Or, Always put the mower on the driveway to fill it with gas. There's a danger of fire if we work in the garage next to the heating unit, and spilling gas on the lawn kills the grass.*

Make the steps of your demonstration clear and complete. Both adults and children learn best when you present each step in chronological order. Often, someone with experience leaves out steps that seem obvious, making assumptions about what others know. Ironically, someone new to a task, who must think about each step and consider recent mistakes, demonstrates more thoroughly. When working with preschoolers, include only two or three steps. Introduce words such as *before* and *after* to help them understand sequence.

I hired a group of temporary employees to prepare a mass mailing, and I planned their procedure carefully. When they arrived, I slowly demonstrated what they were to do. "First, fold the letter up from the bottom and crease that bottom fold. Then, fold the top down and crease it. Insert the letter, bottom fold first, into the envelope, and seal the envelope. Next, sort the letters and bag them in mail bags labeled by zip code."

Then, I left for the day. The next morning the mailbags were piled on my desk with a note from the Postmaster that said, "Anybody knows that you must put stamps on letters before you mail them!" Though I had provided stamps, I had said nothing about them.

—————————————————————————————————*L.C.D.*

3. Two-way participation keeps the learner involved.

After demonstrating each step, stop and allow the learner to try it. *Riley, go ahead and set up that side of the room, while I get the handbooks.* Or, *Here's the gas can, Chris. Pour the gas in here.* Both adults and children learn best by doing. As they practice, they take ownership of the steps and build their self-confidence.

Showing someone skills at the end of a workday or while waiting for the school bus does not allow adequate time for hands-on involvement. Likewise, seeing and practicing a procedure too far in advance prevents direct application. Time your demonstration so that the learner can participate immediately, such as when you and the new employee want to send a fax or when you and your daughter prepare to clean the aquarium.

Occasionally, you must teach a new skill without an opportunity for hands-on demonstrating: when a telecommuting employee e-mails for instructions on completing the new expense report or when the college student calls for directions on roasting the Thanksgiving turkey. In such cases, structure by asking the employee or child to recall similar past experiences, such as how you demonstrated completing previous reports or how Grandmother prepared her turkey. When the employee or child has no prior experience, you can create a mental picture by describing the new skill. When equipment in the field malfunctions, a manager on a radio may talk a worker through shutting it off. When a teenager has a flat tire, a parent may describe by cell phone how to change it.

The following examples and worksheets offer questions to think about when you plan your next demonstration.

DEMONSTRATING EXPECTATIONS - EXAMPLES

1. TEACH TO THE LEARNER'S SKILL LEVEL.

Manager: *Some nights Mr. Martinez works late and needs copies. He already knows how to use the copy machine but gets frustrated easily when the paper gets stuck. Frequently, he leaves it that way for the morning crew to fix. He needs to learn how to clear the paper.*

Parent: *Ryan, my three-year-old, needs to begin helping with household chores. He is very interested when I unload the dishwasher, and it is safe for him to handle anything that is not breakable. Maybe I'll start with the silverware.*

2. TALK ABOUT YOUR EXPECTATIONS AS YOU SHOW THE STEPS.

Manager: *Mr. Martinez, let me show you how to clear the machine when the paper sticks. Then others can make copies when they come in the next day. Just release this side door catch, and slide the paper tray out. Then raise the top and reach down here for the jammed paper.*

Parent: *Ryan, I see you are interested in helping unload the dishwasher. From now on you can empty all the silverware out of the dishwasher. When you take out the spoons, they go in this tray . . . .*

3. TWO-WAY PARTICIPATION KEEPS THE LEARNER INVOLVED.

Manager: *I'll release the side door catch and get the paper tray. See if you can clear the paper that's stuck in it now.*

Parent: *I'll put the tray on your little table, and you put each piece of silverware in the right place.*

DEMONSTRATING EXPECTATIONS - PRACTICE

1. TEACH TO THE LEARNER'S SKILL LEVEL.

Manager: _____

_____

_____

Parent: _____

_____

_____

2. TALK ABOUT YOUR EXPECTATIONS AS YOU SHOW THE STEPS.

Manager: _____

_____

_____

Parent: _____

_____

_____

3. TWO-WAY PARTICIPATION KEEPS THE LEARNER INVOLVED.

Manager: _____

_____

_____

Parent: _____

_____

_____

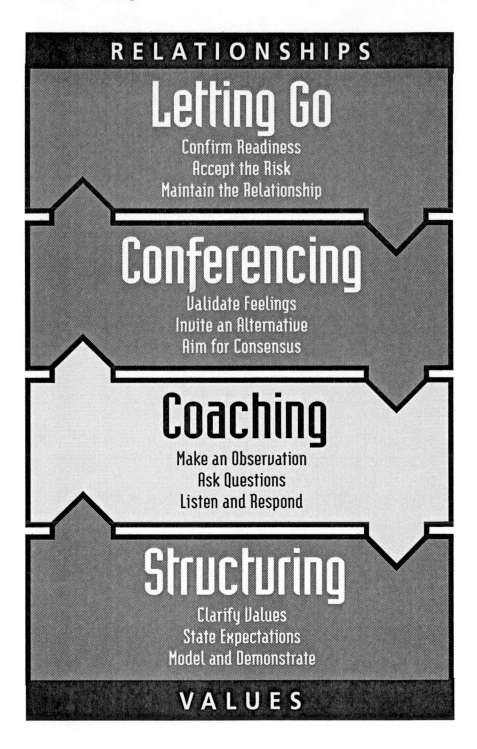

RELATIONSHIPS

Letting Go
Confirm Readiness
Accept the Risk
Maintain the Relationship

Conferencing
Validate Feelings
Invite an Alternative
Aim for Consensus

Coaching
Make an Observation
Ask Questions
Listen and Respond

Structuring
Clarify Values
State Expectations
Model and Demonstrate

VALUES

CHAPTER THREE

Coaching

Through **coaching**, the mentor enables the employee or child to choose **how** to perform. When she exhibits independent techniques and skills, your focus shifts from communicating performance expectations to encouraging skill development. You still maintain **why** your organization or family holds certain values and **what** expected behavior those values require. You support her personal techniques as long as behavior reflects established values and expectations.

YOUR COACHING SCORE

Items four through six on the self-tests in Chapter One indicate your approach to **coaching**. Transfer your answers from those items to the box on the next page. Add your scores vertically. Compare your coaching scores to the descriptions of the four coaching styles that follow.

Items Related to Coaching

SELF-TEST FOR WORK

4.	c _____	a _____	d _____	b _____
5.	a _____	c _____	b _____	d _____
6.	b _____	d _____	a _____	c _____
TOTALS	_____	_____	_____	_____
	BOSS	MANIPULATOR	MARTYR	MENTOR

SELF-TEST FOR HOME

4.	c _____	a _____	d _____	b _____
5.	a _____	c _____	b _____	d _____
6.	b _____	d _____	a _____	c _____
TOTALS	_____	_____	_____	_____
	BOSS	MANIPULATOR	MARTYR	MENTOR

HOW EACH STYLE COACHES

The **boss** fails to comprehend the need to coach. She assumes that others do not have the capacity to develop and improve their own skills. This belief drives her to tell employees and children what to do. She observes their behavior only to assure compliance with her instructions. The boss manager may resort to demeaning questions that force others to justify their actions. *I told you what to do. Why on earth did you do it that way?* When the boss parent dictates without listening to the child's perspective, she fuels resentment that may explode with time. *I don't want to know what happened, just apologize.* Because the boss does not trust the innate ability of people to learn and grow, she perpetuates their dependence on her rather than encouraging them to develop their own skills.

The **manipulator's** interpretation of coaching stems from his belief that motivation requires incentives. He accepts the potential of others to learn and wants them to be responsible. Yet, he assumes they will do neither without the right reward or threat. He observes, questions, and listens only to determine the "best" incentive, not realizing that this diverts attention from the value of the behavior. The manipulator manager emphasizes the promotion an employee will receive for learning the new computer program. *If you'll learn that computer program, I will schedule you for a promotion.* He mistakenly responds with a reward and not with the program's timesaving advantage to the employee. The manipulator parent believes behavior will improve with ever-increasing rewards. Eventually, the child becomes saturated. The parent describes her as "not motivated." *We've even offered to pay her to complete her schoolwork, but she just isn't interested. What will it take to motivate her?*

The **martyr** has no internal strength for coaching. She shares only positive observations, avoids correcting people, and excuses poor performance because she wants others to like her. When told to coach an employee, the martyr manager usually blames "them" or the home office. *They say you have to change.* This implies that the manager would allow the status quo, even though she may routinely complain about the employee's behavior. The martyr parent hopes that her child will behave but uses questions to gain compliance rather than understanding. *Honey, would you please get off the lady's couch?* Scotty, by now a confirmed couch-jumper, ignores her, and she makes excuses. *Scotty just has so much energy.*

The **mentor** coaches from the structure of values and expectations. As a coach, he begins to transfer the responsibility for skill development to the employee or child. He shares his knowledge and experience through active teaching that encourages hands-on learning. The mentor coach makes observations and asks questions to encourage personal techniques. *I heard your customer complain. How do you suggest we satisfy her?* He guides emerging skills with proactive responses rather than reactive comments. *What is your plan for covering your paper route while you are on your camping trip?* As a coach, he focuses on results through developing self-direction rather than exerting control.

COACHING AS A STRATEGY

Coaching begins when the mentor stops demonstrating, and only the employee or child performs: entering payroll data, leading the safety meeting, holding the toothbrush, or turning the key in the ignition. However, a mentor must remember that the skills and techniques belong to the employee or child.

> *During a management training session, a former Big-12 university women's basketball coach described an experience common to all coaches. "The score is tied with thirty seconds left to play. You signal your players to call a time-out. As they gather at the bench, you realize that your success as a coach rests on how well those five people perform in the next thirty seconds. At this point, every coach realizes: 'I can't play!'*
>
> *"Urgently, you focus on what strategies and encouragement to share. When the buzzer sounds and play resumes, your players must rely on their own skills and judgment, molded by your guidance. You stand aside and watch. You wonder if you said enough or too much, if you focused on the most appropriate skills, or if you shared as much of yourself as you might have."*
>
> —*L.C.D.*

The coaching strategy requires the mentor to focus on values and expectations rather than on control as the employee or child begins to develop personal techniques. The nurse manager reinforces the hospital's value of keeping accurate records when she explains the expectations for charting. *Each patient's chart must be complete before you leave for the day.* She models her personal approach to charting by updating patient information throughout her shift. However, she must focus on results and not her frustration, as her employee waits until the end of the day to begin his charts.

The parent demonstrates mowing the lawn for her thirteen-year-old son. *We want the lawn mowed evenly, so always go back and forth.* As the boy begins mowing from north to south, the parent observes that his way differs from her own east to west preference. Yet, her son's technique meets her family's value of neighborhood pride and expectation for an attractive lawn.

> *Each time Murray asked three-year-old Shawna to pick up her toys, she responded with a tantrum. He agreed to coach her about finding other ways to express her feelings. I encouraged Murray to accept whatever alternative Shawna selected. If it worked for her, it needed to work for him as well. When they discussed her tantrums, she identified other ways she might express her frustration.*
>
> *The next time Shawna threw herself on the floor kicking and screaming, Murray reminded her, "Shawna, what else could you do to feel better?" Shawna stopped and looked at Murray. She got up, walked into the kitchen, put on a candy necklace, and picked up her toys.*
>
> — *C.C.M.*

The coaching strategy depends on an encouraging and conversational relationship, aimed at participatory self-discovery. Coaching feels supportive and nonthreatening because the mentor builds on strengths rather than weaknesses. *You are good with details, so making a list of the steps involved in this task is a good idea.* She guides with specific and descriptive observations. *Okay, you dropped that fly ball. You looked away before it got to your glove.* To encourage him to think, the mentor employs more questions than statements. *What can you do differently next time?* She listens and accepts his perspective. Her constructive responses guide him as he learns how to develop skills that meet performance expectations.

Twelve-year-old Jacob badly wanted a pet hedgehog. His mother told him that the family could not have another pet until he fulfilled his current responsibility to the family dog. "What do you think you could do, Jacob, to help you remember to give Sparky fresh water every day?"

Thinking for a few moments, Jacob replied, "I know! I'll tape a note on my bathroom mirror so that when I brush my teeth in the morning I'll remember to change Sparky's water." Jacob got a notepad, wrote CHANGE DOG WATER, and taped it in the middle of his bathroom mirror. Within a few weeks, the family welcomed a hedgehog named Barney.

—— C.C.M.

The manager begins coaching dialogue with an observation about a developing situation. *Sam, it sounds as if Mr. Edwards is angry about the supplies we delivered earlier today.* To help the employee further clarify the problem, she asks a question. *What upset him?* After listening to Sam's perspective of the issues, she restates the organization's expectations and involves him in the process of satisfying the customer. *We always want to satisfy our customers. What do you think you might say to him?* She helps him talk through his upcoming conversation and supports his plan of action. *That sounds as if it will work.*

Walking through the plant, Colin noticed that Vincent had his safety glasses off again. "Hey, Vince," he called. "Those glasses aren't doing you any good on the bench."

"Aw, Colin," Vincent growled. "I just forget to put 'em on."

"Your safety is the most important thing to all of us, Vincent, and that includes protecting your eyes while you work. Now you've got to wear

*your glasses all the time, so how can you make yourself remember?"
Colin pressed.*

*After an awkward pause, Vincent suggested, "I guess I could hang them
on the handle of my machine when I leave. Then they'd be right there
every time I start up."*

"Sounds like a winner, Vince. Give it a try!"

—*L.C.D.*

For parents, starting with an observation avoids the perception
of parental control. *It sounds like you and your college roommate
are not getting along. What seems to create the most difficulty?* After
listening to her daughter's side of the story, the parent reminds her
of relevant expectations and helps her focus on how she can talk to
her roommate. *It is important to try to work things out. How can you
better explain to her how you feel?* Helpful responses support the
child's view of herself as self-reliant. *Asking her point of view sounds
like a good place to start.*

Managers and parents continually look for informal and inci-
dental opportunities to coach, even in the elevator between meetings
or in the car on the way to school. At times, coaching during an
activity helps the employee or child determine what to do next.
Coaching also can serve as debriefing immediately after an incident
or evolve comfortably during a routine conversation.

*Jessica was eager to share a recent insight. "My six-year-old son, Marco,
was putting together a list of favorite baseball players, and he asked me
how to spell 'Fraiser.' I was busy preparing dinner and was mentally
sidetracked. Before thinking, I started spelling it for him. When I 'came
to' and realized what I was doing, I backtracked and said 'I'll sound it
out, and you see what letter you think it is.'"*

— *C.C.M.*

Introducing too many issues at once causes the employee or child to feel nagged, overwhelmed, or discouraged. Although the coach may notice several coachable issues, she deals with only one at a time, allowing self-confidence to increase with mastery of one task before tackling the next.

Managers and parents coach to improve both technical and behavioral skills. Technical coaching issues usually relate to well-defined tasks, such as making a sale, repairing equipment, tying shoes, or changing spark plugs. Behavioral coaching presents a greater challenge and requires more courage because it relates to emotional and interpersonal skills: how to listen patiently to coworkers, dress professionally, react to a customer complaint, cooperate with a playmate, return a stolen item, or face others after losing an election.

Five-year-old Rob and his friend Austin were playing in the family room, when Jill heard Austin scream. Going to the boys, Jill put her arm around Austin as she said, "Look how upset Austin is. What happened?"

Austin sobbed, "Rob twisted my arm."

Coaching Rob, Jill asked, "If you hurt him, you need to figure out a way to make him feel better. What can you do?"

"Sorry," Rob muttered in an off-handed manner.

"I'm not sure that apologizing makes it better for Austin," Jill observed. "He is still crying. What would Austin say if you asked him how to make it better?"

"How can I make it better, Austin?" Rob asked.

Austin stopped crying, thought for a moment, and grinned. "Kiss my hand." Rob kissed his hand, Austin beamed, and the boys resumed their play.

— *C.C.M.*

In an effort to avoid tension, managers and parents sometimes choose to overlook inappropriate behavior. Often, managers let poor performance slide without giving the employee an opportunity to change. Having allowed an intolerable situation to continue, the manager then sees termination as the only option. Sometimes, parents, too, ignore misbehavior and miss an opportunity to promote a child's skill development. When managers and parents fail to coach, their employees and children may experience confusion, develop bad habits, or become defensive. *Why didn't you tell me before?* Or, *Why didn't you help me?* Risking momentary resistance or resentment, trustworthy coaches respond in an honest and respectful manner.

> *In a small-town office of a government agency, many employees were related to each other. Managers maintained that "close relationships" would make conversations about poor employee performance uncomfortable. Finally, one manager took issue with the rest by saying, "You know, I don't see it that way. If my neighbor's son drives too fast in front of my house, I say to myself 'That kid's going to have a wreck one of these days.' But I don't do or say anything else because I'm not that close to him. However, if my son drives too fast, I sit him down and talk to him. Even if it makes us both uncomfortable, I do it because I love him and care about him. Being close and caring means you have to talk about tough issues."*
>
> —L.C.D.

Coaching at Work

Acknowledging the need to coach redefines the manager's relationship with his employees. The manager supports employees' growth and encourages ownership of behavior. *You've created a clever jingle. This is an opportunity for you to make the presentation to the client.* Coaching begins to transfer responsibility to employees and relieves the manager of making every decision. The manager, however, may wonder what remains for him to do. In fact, his daily routine will change when he sees himself as a coach: willingly describing his observations about performance, encouraging new skills when the opportunity arises, and involving others in defining their own approach to work. His value to the organization increases as he facilitates others' decision-making processes rather than serving as their primary decision-maker.

Some managers resist coaching because of the perceived time involved. As with any new skill, coaching initially does take longer. Although awkward at first, productive coaching can occur comfortably within daily conversations as the manager practices.

> *"She's gonna be mad," Raul protested to Mindy. He had stopped by Mindy's call center office to describe his research into a customer's problem. "Our system won't do what she wants. You want to call her back to tell her?"*
>
> *"No, you talked to her and know all the issues. You can call her," Mindy encouraged. "Let's talk about what you'll say. How might you start?"*
>
> *"Well, I guess I should thank her for calling the problem to our attention," Raul began.*
>
> *"So you'll express our appreciation. Do you think you should apologize?"*
>
> *"No," he thought aloud. "I'm not going to apologize for our system, but I could apologize for her inconvenience."*
>
> *"What else will you say?" Mindy prompted as she continued to coach him toward a successful call.*
>
> —————————————————————————————*L.C.D.*

Most managers would prefer to coach about technical skills, such as following procedures or completing forms, rather than about behavioral practices, such as listening to others in a team meeting or restricting personal phone calls. Personal hygiene issues rank as almost every manager's most difficult coaching topic. Nevertheless, a conscientious coach must deal with any issue that detracts from an employee's success.

Coaching at Home

When parents view themselves as supportive partners in the child's skill development, they encourage self-direction. They coach proactively rather than react to perceived misbehavior. However, it takes patience to watch a three-year-old learn to empty the trash, an eight-year-old try to mop the floor, or a teenager begin to drive the car. Often, parents find it easier and less stressful to do the task themselves or avoid the issue rather than take time to make observations about progress and discuss techniques. Yet, if parents fail to coach, they increasingly give orders to children, trying to gain compliance and control.

> *Latanya's parents continually told her to pick up her toys. Frequently, when they reminded her, eight-year-old Latanya would reply, "Boring!" One night, finding toys scattered all over, Latanya's dad angrily started putting them in bags.*
>
> *Latanya cried, "Not my Esmarelda costume! I didn't think you were going to do it! It would be easier to hang up my purse than to put it in the bag!"*
>
> *Latanya's dad explained, "But, Latanya, we gave you so many chances!"*
>
> *"Yes," replied Latanya, "Thirteen."*
>
> —————————————————————— *C.C.M.*

Sometimes when a parent and child battle for control, attributing a positive intent to the child avoids a circular argument. When three-year-old Slade stood on the bathroom counter and looked defiant, his father playfully lifted him down while observing *I see you want to be tall. You are getting so big!* Saying *You're on that counter again. What did I tell you?* perpetuates the focus on control. With children, sometimes physically supporting the expectation instead of discussing it will make the point. When four-year-old Ishmael ran away from his mother through an unknown creek, she engaged his cooperation by taking his hand and observing *I see you want to explore. Let's go together to see if there are fish over here!* Restoring their relationship will allow her to ask him later how he will remember to wait for an adult.

> *Peter and Serena, both four-and-a-half, were neighbors and best play-mates who had earned enough trust to play unsupervised. When Peter's mother, Jean, came to get Peter at Serena's house, the parents heard noises from upstairs. Opening the door to the master bedroom, they were greeted with the sight of hundreds of goldfish crackers all over and under the bed, dresser, nightstands, chairs, and in the bathroom as well. The fish crackers were in every possible form: whole, halves, pieces, and crushed.*
>
> *Too upset to say more, Jean firmly told Peter, "We have some cleaning up to do before we go home to discuss what happened here." Together, they stripped the bedspread, took it outside to shake the crackers off, and cleaned up the room. When they got home, Jean suggested that they sit on the stairs and talk. Jean later confided, "I was amazed that I maintained my composure and muzzled my anger, but it was my determination to talk with him about this that kept me somewhat in line. I knew that if I blew my lid, he would follow suit and we would get nowhere." Following is the conversation that took place.*

Jean: *Peter, there were fish crackers all over that room! What happened at Serena's house?*

Peter: *Well, Serena and I were playing dog-fish.*

Jean: *Just what exactly is dog-fish, and how do you play it?*

Peter: *Serena and I reached up high in her pantry and got the big box of goldfish crackers. We decided to take it upstairs, and Bucky-dog followed us.*

Jean: Then what happened?

Peter: We just closed the door and opened the box. We threw crackers in the air, and Bucky-dog chased them all around the room. They crunched when he ran over them! Bucky-dog barked and kept running around, so we kept throwing them in the air.

Jean: How do you think this game made Bucky feel?

Peter: Scared and frightened.

Jean: And how do you think Serena's parents feel about this game and the mess it made?

Peter: Mad. Upset at the mess. Not happy.

Jean: I know you and Serena like to play together, and I know you like for Bucky-dog to play with you, too. It is understandable that you were hungry, and it was fun to take such a huge box of fish crackers into a secret place where you could eat them and play together.

Peter: Uh-huh.

Jean: You need to show Serena's parents that you two can be trusted to play together again. What can you do?

Peter: Well, I can make sure Bucky-dog isn't shut into a room with us anymore so that he can leave the room if he wants to. I can apologize to Serena's parents for making a mess and for wasting a box of goldfish crackers. I think it would also be a good idea if Serena and I didn't play alone without an adult.

Jean: Those are some very worthwhile ideas you have, Peter. What can we do now since we know Bucky was frightened, a box of goldfish crackers was wasted, and Serena's house was a mess?

Peter: Well, I could apologize to Bucky-dog and tell him I'm sorry for frightening him. Then I could also say 'I'm sorry' to Serena's parents for making a mess and doing something wrong like we did. But I did already help clean up the crackers.

Jean: What can we do about the box of goldfish crackers?

Peter: We can buy a new box.

Jean: Okay. How are we going to buy a new box?

Peter: We can go to the store. They sell those big boxes at the warehouse store.

Jean: And how are we going to pay for the crackers?

Peter: With money.

Jean: And where are we going to get the money?

Peter: From your wallet, Mom.

Jean: I don't think it's right for Mommy to pay for the crackers since I wasn't the one who used them up. Do you have any other ideas?

Peter: We could use my money out of my piggy bank then.

Jean: So we will go to the store and buy a new box of goldfish crackers with your money, and then you can take them over to Serena's house when you go to apologize.

Jean concluded, "I finally exhaled. The ordeal was over. I sat there with Peter at my side and told him how proud I was of him for talking about the entire situation with me. He acknowledged how it made everyone feel, how he learned never to play dog-fish again, but most importantly, that we could sit and calmly discuss the situation."

"As I watched Peter climb onto his bike with a big box of goldfish crackers tied to the handlebars and zoom around the corner to Serena's house, I realized what a valuable lesson I had learned as a parent. I also chuckled silently, knowing Serena's parents probably were not ready to see another goldfish cracker!"

— *C.C.M.*

COACHING SKILLS

The coaching strategy shifts your emphasis from structuring performance expectations to encouraging the skill development of your employee or child. As a mentor, you coach when you practice the following three skills.

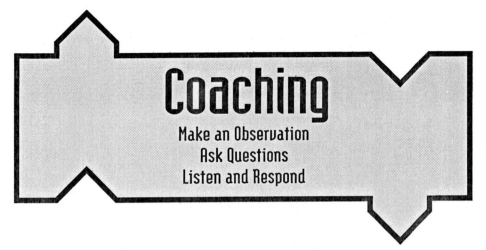

Coaching

Make an Observation
Ask Questions
Listen and Respond

Coaching Skill: Make an Observation

Observations reflect the values and expectations of your organization or family and have both a visual and a verbal component. For example, if your organization expects professional attire, noticing an employee's starched shirt and pressed jacket is the visual part of the observation. Commenting on how his attire relates to the organization's expectations adds the verbal portion. *Charlie, your shirt and jacket look sharp!* At home, seeing a child shove dirty clothes under the bed may collide with your family's expectations. Once you observe this, begin a coaching conversation by describing what you see. *I see dirty clothes under the bed.*

What Do You See?

Focus your attention on incidents that relate to what you expect, not those that simply bother you. Nelson may have a cluttered workspace, but disregard it if he works away from the customer contact area. As long as he can find what he needs, leave him alone. Your teenage daughter may enjoy primping in front of the mirror. If it bothers you to watch, turn your attention elsewhere.

"I've got her now," gloated Raylene, the credit union supervisor, into my phone. "I've followed Gladys all day and made notes about everything she gossiped about! Now that I've documented everything, like you said, I'm ready to talk to her."

Raylene had come to me for advice about how to deal with Gladys's poor performance and low work output. I had urged her to record her observations before confronting Gladys. Convinced that Gladys's irritating gossip was the issue, she had carefully noted Gladys's every story for an entire day instead of measuring her work output.

—L.C.D.

Observe both the task itself and the process involved. This will give you a more well-rounded picture. A deli manager observes both the quality of the deli sandwich and the time it took to prepare it. A parent observes that the child both returned the neighbor's dish and said thank you.

Frequently, managers and parents make the mistake of reacting too soon. Stop to assess the relevance of what you observe before you say anything to your employee or child. You may feel stifled at the notion of not talking right away. However, organizing your thoughts increases your coaching effectiveness.

Grassa had explained to her nine-year-old daughter, Elana, why she should not touch old chewing gum that was stuck to the sidewalk. Grassa told me, "I realized that children need time to change gears before stopping, and I knew she might touch it one more time. When I observed Elana touching the gum after I had just talked with her about it, I had to remember to take a deep breath!"

— C.C.M.

Accurate and helpful observations require commitment of your time. As a manager, if you become preoccupied with your own tasks, you fail to notice what goes on around you. Hovering over your computer with your back to the door separates you from daily life in your organization. *I was so busy today that I never noticed what anyone else did.* As a parent, observing requires your full attention, even though you may prefer to continue reading the paper as your child describes his day. You will find it difficult to understand the complexity of children's behavior when busy with your own agenda. *I got so much done today. The kids played in the basement all morning. I never even heard them.*

Look for additional information that may not seem apparent at first. Suppose you observe the conference room in disarray. Knowing that Charles used it yesterday, you may be tempted to accuse him before discovering that the boss had a seminar there last night. When you hear your toddler cry, avoid assuming that your preschooler disturbed her. Before yelling accusations from the other room, check the situation yourself.

> *Carole and two-year-old Henry were visiting their friends, Suzy and her son Mitchell, for a play date. Despite the fact that Henry often communicated with his friends by hitting rather than with words, Carole was enjoying adult conversation with Suzy, while Henry and Mitchell had a snack and played in the other room.*
>
> *When Mitchell cried that Henry had hit him, Carole immediately rushed in, picked up Henry, and took him home as punishment. Later in the day, Henry trustingly asked Carole, "Why did Mitchell eat my food?" Carole realized that without observing the situation, she had made a hasty judgment.*
>
> — *C.C.M.*

As you observe how your employee or child fulfills your expectations, you may feel stunned by his unique approach to a task that you perform in another way. It may seem strange to see an employee standing to lead a staff meeting instead of sitting like you do. Or, it may surprise you to observe your child washing the car before vacuuming it instead of afterward. Realize that his way might be successful, too.

> *Chloe had placed "Be Quiet" signs throughout the business office, convinced that employee talk from cubicle to cubicle was the cause of her team's high error rate. She explained her reasoning: "People make more mistakes when there are distracting noises around, so if they'll just be quiet they'll make fewer mistakes."*
>
> *When I talked to her employees, they told me that Chloe is the one who must have quiet. They explained that they talked between the cubicles to help each other understand procedures, since there were no written guidelines. A lack of specific procedures was the real cause of their errors.*
>
> —*L.C.D.*

What Do You Say?

As a mentor, starting a conversation about someone's performance can affect your entire relationship. Even a well-intentioned manager or parent risks sounding accusatory. Yet, failure to address ongoing issues does not offer an employee or child opportunity to change.

To open a coaching conversation safely, simply make a factual statement describing what you observed. Starting in this way creates a nonthreatening opportunity for discussion and sharing. *You seem hesitant to take on the new assignment* begins a conversation about a skill needing further improvement. *You finished your homework before dinner* offers an opportunity to talk about progress in skill development. Begin your conversation soon after your observation and before bad habits develop. Conduct your coaching conversation in private for a comfortable, supportive discussion.

As you practice making an observation, use the following checklist to guide you.

Making an Observation

1. Provide objective, unemotional information.

2. Describe specific facts and details.

3. Communicate in a straightforward yet tactful manner.

1. Provide objective, unemotional information.

An objective observation does not focus on good or bad, right or wrong, but simply identifies actions or conditions. *Sally, this memo has three typos in it* invites discussion in more neutral terms than *Well, you ruined another memo.* Unbiased observations avoid blame: *I see the apple juice spilled* instead of *When will you ever learn to pour something without spilling it?* Effective coaches begin with a conscious effort to describe what they observe. *Twice you interrupted the client while he was talking.* Or, *Your sister just ran to her room and slammed the door.*

Often, coaches mistakenly make assumptions about motives, jump to conclusions, and let personal biases stand in the way. *You interrupted the client because you didn't like his ideas.* Or, *What did you do now to hurt your sister's feelings?* Assuming you know someone else's reasons or actions creates immediate resentment. *You borrowed the Jones file yesterday, and you probably didn't return it to the files.* Directing your teenager to *Put your dish in the kitchen* as he heads that way, dish in hand, provokes his hostility.

> *While coaching Denise, she told me about an employee who frequently recorded incorrect information in customers' files. Denise confided, "I'm not ready to talk to him about it yet because I'm not mad enough." She mistakenly believed that feeling anger was a prerequisite for discussing an employee's errors.*
>
> —*L.C.D.*

Emotion impedes an open dialogue. Facing your anger, stress, or negative feelings about a person requires you to reframe your observation unemotionally. Prepare for a respectful coaching conversation by waiting until you calm down. Focus the conversation on what happened rather than on your feelings. Try *The boxes aren't packed for my ten o'clock presentation* rather than *I've got too much stress to deal with these boxes not being packed!* Or try, *Your bike is in the yard, and it's raining* rather than *I get so mad when I see that bike left in the rain.*

When you provide objective information consistently, you concentrate attention on a specific behavior. However, when you observe the behavior on one day and ignore it the next, your inconsistency diminishes the focus.

Cherie was frustrated with four-year-old David, who would frequently run "wild" around the living room. After careful observation, she noticed that these episodes intensified after David watched a television cartoon about powerful superheroes. At a calm moment, Cherie shared with David her observation that his wild behavior seemed to occur after he watched these programs.

A few days later, after a cartoon, David was racing around the living room. Cherie pointed out, "David, this is the kind of behavior we were talking about." David immediately stopped, looked around in surprise, and walked off to play in another room.

— *C.C.M.*

2. Describe specific facts and details.

Begin coaching with a precise description of what you observed. Instead of *You made a good presentation,* specify what made the presentation effective. *Your use of PowerPoint really helped the audience understand your key points.* Instead of saying *The hamster cage needs work,* say *I see that your hamster is out of water.*

Avoid the tendency to use phrases such as *You always* or *You never. You always forget to turn off the copy machine when you leave* overgeneralizes, but *I noticed that the copy machine was on after you left yesterday* describes exact information. *You never introduce me to your friends* accuses, but *There were two boys at the party whom I don't know* points toward a solution.

> *Kristy had three school-age daughters. Her home became very hectic in the afternoons after school. Kristy told me, "I read a book and learned to respond to any misbehavior by saying '1-2-3!' It's great! I don't have to say anything else. By the time I get to three, they'll do what I want!"*
>
> *A month later Kristy returned, puzzled by the need to keep saying "1-2-3!" and by her daughters' continued misbehavior and increasing hostility.*
>
> — *C.C.M.*

Common phrases, such as *Good job* or *Well done*, though positive, provide no specific information about what to do next time. A more helpful observation relates current behavior to a specific expectation. *I found the financial information I needed because you filed it with the project report* identifies an appropriate practice for the future. The employee draws his own conclusion that this action constitutes a "good job."

With children, popular comments such as *Good boy* inappropriately focus the child's attention on the state of "being good." When told *Good boy* when he puts the cap back on the toothpaste, the child may worry about not "being good" on a day when he forgets to replace the cap. Some children, to the chagrin of their parents, then test a variety of behaviors to define "good" or "bad."

3. Communicate in a straightforward yet tactful manner.

Mentor coaches walk a fine line between making candid observations and saying hurtful things. In an effort to avoid offending, you may feel that you should downplay your comments. Yet, words or phrases such as *sometimes, maybe, a little bit,* and *might,* trivialize your observation and allow the employee or child to disregard it. *You might want to pay a little bit more attention.* Have courage to make an honest observation, delivered in a caring manner. *You need to pay more attention.*

Spiteful comments bring on an argument rather than a constructive coaching conversation. Loaded words, such as *mean, lazy,* and *rude,* judge character and provide no basis for discussion aimed at improving a specific skill. They simply lead to defensiveness or hurt feelings and deflect attention from the intent of your observation.

> *The CEO was trying to inspire an overweight supervisor to accept a promotion with more responsibility. In an effort to minimize her current position, he observed, "You could just stay where you are, in your little office, fat, dumb, and . . . ."*
>
> *He paused, embarrassed by what he had said and concluded with, "Any other person would jump at the chance to further their career." As a coach, his tactlessness caused the supervisor not only to feel insulted but also to resent his opinion of her current achievements.*
>
> —*L.C.D.*

As you plan your coaching conversation, use the following examples and worksheets to practice making observations.

MAKING AN OBSERVATION AT WORK - EXAMPLES

What is Your Organization's Value?

Prompt customer service

What is Your Organization's Expectation?

Front office employees must greet customers as soon as they enter the front office.

What Do You See?

Nancy finishes typing orders or filing, while customers wait in the front office.

What Do You Say?

"Nancy, earlier today I noticed two customers waiting in the front office."

Check Your Observation. Does it:

☐ Provide unemotional, objective information?

☐ Give specific facts and details?

☐ Communicate in a straightforward and tactful manner?

MAKING AN OBSERVATION AT HOME - EXAMPLES

What is Your Family's Value?

Responsibility for personal belongings

What is Your Family's Expectation?

Toys will be put away before bedtime.

What Do You See?

Three-year-old Calvin has been playing horse farm. Before bedtime, he puts all the horses back in the toy barn without reminding.

What Do You Say?

"Calvin, it's nearly bedtime, and you put your horses back in the barn all by yourself!"

Check Your Observation. Does it:

☐ Provide unemotional, objective information?

☐ Give specific facts and details?

☐ Communicate in a straightforward and tactful manner?

MAKING AN OBSERVATION AT WORK - PRACTICE

What is Your Organization's Value?

_____

_____

_____

What is Your Organization's Expectation?

_____

_____

_____

What Do You See?

_____

_____

_____

What Do You Say?

_____

_____

_____

Check Your Observation. Does it:

- ☐ Provide unemotional, objective information?
- ☐ Give specific facts and details?
- ☐ Communicate in a straightforward and tactful manner?

MAKING AN OBSERVATION AT HOME - PRACTICE

What is Your Family's Value?

_____

_____

_____

What is Your Family's Expectation?

_____

_____

_____

What Do You See?

_____

_____

_____

What Do You Say?

_____

_____

_____

Check Your Observation. Does it:

☐ Provide unemotional, objective information?

☐ Give specific facts and details?

☐ Communicate in a straightforward and tactful manner?

Coaching Skill: Ask Questions

In your role as a mentor coach, you ask questions to establish an accepting climate for the views of the employee or child. Your questions imply your willingness to listen. Throughout the coaching conversation, they encourage dialogue that helps her determine how to improve her skills.

Especially remember to ask questions at two critical points in the coaching conversation. At the beginning of the conversation, make an **observation** about her performance, then ask questions to clarify her perspective. After listening to your employee or child describe her point of view, state your **expectation** followed by other questions.

Questions that follow **observations** encourage your employee or child to share her perspective. *What is your understanding?* Or, *What is your take on that?* Or, *How did that happen?* Without your questions, she may not recognize the opportunity or necessity to tell her point of view. Her input will offer additional information and help clarify the issues. *Wilna, you have been trying the new procedure for a week now. Is the new format working for you?* Managers and parents, believing in their own singular perspective, frequently neglect to recognize that employees and children have valid ideas and opinions. *Your grade on this math test is lower than usual. What do you think is causing you trouble?*

Claudia, a supervisor at a state university, came to me because her employees were not "motivated." As we talked, I began to ask her about her staff, "What do they like or enjoy?"

"I don't have any idea," she said.

I suggested that she take one hour to visit with each of her seven employees before our next meeting. Her assignment was to ask only two questions, "How is your job going?" and "How could I make it better?" She was to take notes and listen intently. When we met again, she brought numerous pages about each person's interests and needs, and was amazed at how "motivated" the staff had become.

—————————————————————————————*L.C.D.*

After you state an **expectation**, ask a question to encourage personal techniques and self-direction. *What are you going to do differently?* Or, *How can you remember to do that?* Or, *Where are you going to start?* Ask only one question at a time, and pause to hear the response. Asking more than one allows the other person to select a question to answer, to respond only to the last question, or to feel overwhelmed. Most managers and parents talk too much, taking ownership away from employees and children. Just ask and wait.

Weston came home from kindergarten and shared with his mom that in the upcoming music concert he was expected to put a crown on Jamar's head. Weston told his mom that he was really nervous about doing this job.

"So your job is to put the crown on Jamar's head," his mom said. "I can hear how anxious you are about that. What kinds of things can you do to help yourself feel better about it?" Weston dictated a list of "possible solutions":

1. *Move to Siberia.*
2. *Take five deep breaths before putting it on his head.*
3. *Somebody else could put the crown on Jamar's head.*
4. *Stay home with the baby-sitter.*
5. *Watch the concert from the audience.*
6. *Extra practice.*
7. *Read library book called* Stage Fright.
8. *Bite your tongue.*
9. *Remember that the audience can't see that it is Weston.*

Weston decided to do numbers 6, 7, 8, and 9. He noted that he needed a crown at home for his extra practice and asked Dad to video the concert. Weston and Mom dated and signed his plan.

————————————————————————————— *C.C.M.*

This is an important turning point in the coaching conversation: your question causes the employee or child to realize that she needs to create her own plan. *You need to schedule your work to make sure you meet this deadline. In what way can you do that?* Or, *Remember when we go to church this morning, it is important for you to sit quietly. How can you make sure that you're quiet?*

> *Eldon and Phyllis were concerned about the early morning routine with their seven-year-old daughter, Mia. "We say all the right things. But at eight o'clock when it is time to leave for school and Mia begins to dawdle, we start bossing."*
>
> *Believing that Mia's behavior was an attempt to draw attention away from her younger sister, Phyllis sat down after school with Mia. "Honey, it seems to me that you and I may not be spending as much time together as we used to. Does it seem like that to you, too?"*
>
> *"Well, sometimes," Mia acknowledged.*
>
> *"What kinds of special things could you and I do together?" After a moment, Mia suggested that she and her mom put on their swimsuits, set out their beach towels in Mia's bedroom, and have a "day" at the beach with her Barbies.*
>
> *After their twenty-minute beach party, Phyllis observed, "This was delightful! What can we do tomorrow?"*
>
> — *C.C.M.*

Often parents underestimate their children, thinking that they cannot imagine how to do things differently. Your child will surprise you at her resourcefulness. With toddlers or very young preschoolers, initially you will have to offer suggestions in partnership with the child until she has enough language and experience to brainstorm ideas with you.

Wayne had involved his four-year-old son, Jason, in coaching conversations around various aspects of their family's routines. Jason began to develop confidence and was proud of the fact that he could come up with new ideas and solutions. One night as the family sat down to dinner, Jason sat up straight and announced, "Does anyone have a problem you need for me to solve?"

— C.C.M.

Questions fall into two basic types: closed probes and open probes. **Closed probes** extract a *yes, no,* or short factual response without asking for further discussion. They allow the manager or parent to direct the flow and content of the conversation, but they will not uncover ideas held only by the other person. A series of *yes* answers confirms what you expected. However, a *no* answer will require you to ask more questions.

Use closed probes when you want to verify your perceptions and gather specific information. *Did you tell her?* Or, *Have you offered that?* Or, *Will you go?* They allow you to focus on familiar issues and anticipated answers. *The report is due today. Is it ready?* Or, *The dog looks hungry. Did you feed him?* However, asking a series of closed probes may frustrate you and cause your employee or child to feel badgered or harassed. *The report is due on Friday. Is it ready? Have you mailed it yet? Can you FedEx it? Can you e-mail it?* Or, *The dog looks hungry. Did you feed him? Did you use the new bag of dog food? Did he eat it? Did you give him water?*

Health care professionals learn to diagnose with a series of closed probes designed to uncover predictable symptoms, such as "Can you move it? Does this hurt? Can you stand?" Yet, the use of closed probes in unpredictable, interpersonal situations can be more frustrating than helpful.

Rosalie, an emergency room head nurse, confronted Grant, a recently hired aide, when he arrived late for his shift. "Did you get caught in traffic?" she asked.

"Nope," he answered.

"Run out of gas or sleep late?"

"Huh-uh."

"Well, did you forget to set your alarm?"

"No."

After exhausting all the reasons she could imagine, Rosalie finally gave up and shook her head. "Well, get to work."

—*L.C.D.*

Open probes stimulate thought and encourage conversation. They imply that you intend to listen and accept what you hear. Begin an open probe with such words and phrases as *who, what, when, where, how, in what way,* and *to what extent.* Use open probes when you want to gather information and hear the other person's perspective. *Who was involved? What's going on with that? When will you schedule that? Where are they now? How did she respond when you told her? In what way can you change that? To what extent do you want to be informed?*

Questions that start with *why* can seem to challenge personal motives. To reduce unnecessary defensiveness, try changing *Why did you do that?* to *What is it that caused you to do that?* Or, soften your tone of voice to make the *why* question more acceptable. Statements also can begin discussion. *Tell me about it. Be more specific about what you'll do. Tell me what happened. Give me another example. Tell me about your plan. Describe that for me.* Yet, if the person feels pressed or threatened, using statements to gather information can result in the same reaction elicited by a *why* question.

As a mentor, you will use both closed and open probes. Although closed probes enable you to gather information quickly, they limit the scope of the discussion to your perspective. Open probes uncover more and varied information; however, they may take the conversation in an unanticipated direction. Managers and parents, concerned about losing control, often avoid open probes. In fact, open probes do shift the source of information to the employee or child and force you to deal with whatever information arises.

> *Roger, a manufacturing plant manager, called me with a dilemma. "I put up a suggestion box two weeks ago, and I just opened it today for the first time. I didn't like any of the suggestions, so I threw them away. Now what should I do?"*
>
> *Recognizing that Roger was unwilling to consider his employees' ideas, I responded regretfully, "Take down the box."*
>
> —*L.C.D.*

The employee or child will respond to the tone of your voice and the tone of your question. For example, listen to yourself ask the question *What are you going to do about it?* in an accusatory manner. Then try it in a helpful, supportive tone. If you frame your question in such a way that it makes an assumption, you will evoke more defensiveness. Asking an employee *Did you check with the receptionist?* will likely receive a different kind of response than *Did you even check with the receptionist?* Ask your child *What happened on this French test?* instead of *Why didn't you study for this French test?*

> *Ten-year-old Stevie came home from school and confided in his mother that he had gotten in a fight on the school playground. Using good coaching skills, Bonita listened to his story, responding with observations and questions. Stevie began to talk about other ways he might have handled the situation.*
>
> *When Stevie's dad came home from work, Stevie tried to share the same story with him. Unfortunately, the only question that his dad asked was, "What are you—stupid?"*
>
> — *C.C.M.*

When in a close mentoring relationship with a child, merely making an observation often serves to elicit a response. Pausing after *The cookies are all gone* may begin dialogue better than asking your daughter *Who ate the last cookie?* The question may intensify sibling blaming and rivalry.

Review and practice questioning techniques on the following pages. Remember that your tone of voice can change a question from one that is accusatory to one that is helpful.

ASKING QUESTIONS AT WORK - EXAMPLES

Make Your Observation:

We had eighteen deliveries leave the warehouse this week. Twelve of them left on time; six of them left after their specified delivery date.

What Questions Might Gain the Employee's Perspective?

What's your take on that?

How did that happen?

Did you know six deliveries were late this week?

What is your understanding of how deliveries are scheduled?

What was different between the twelve on-time deliveries and the six late ones?

Who notified the customers with the late deliveries?

State Your Organization's Expectation:

Every delivery needs to leave the warehouse on its specified delivery date.

What Questions Might Encourage the Employee's Skill Development?

How can you make certain the deliveries get out on time?

What can you do if an order simply cannot be filled on time?

How can we use the new routing system to speed our deliveries?

Are we allowing enough time to process each delivery?

Notice the use of closed or open probes.

ASKING QUESTIONS AT HOME - EXAMPLES

Make Your Observation:

I notice you are wearing your sister's new belt.

What Questions Might Gain the Child's Perspective?

How did that happen?

What's the deal?

How come?

Did she give you permission?

What did she say when you asked if you could borrow it?

Tell me how you arranged to borrow it.

State Your Family's Expectation:

You need permission to borrow the personal belongings of family members.

What Questions Might Encourage the Child's Skill Development?

What are you going to do now?

How might you arrange to borrow her belt sometime?

Next time you want to borrow her belt, what will you do?

Do you and your sister have a plan for borrowing from each other?

Notice the use of closed or open probes.

ASKING QUESTIONS AT WORK - PRACTICE

Make Your Observation:

_____

_____

_____

What Questions Might Gain the Employee's Perspective?

_____

_____

_____

_____

_____

_____

State Your Organization's Expectation:

_____

_____

_____

What Questions Might Encourage the Employee's Skill Development?

_____

_____

_____

_____

_____

_____

Notice your use of closed or open probes.

ASKING QUESTIONS AT HOME - PRACTICE

Make Your Observation:

_____

_____

_____

What Questions Might Gain the Child's Perspective?

_____

_____

_____

_____

_____

_____

State Your Family's Expectation:

_____

_____

_____

What Questions Might Encourage the Child's Skill Development?

_____

_____

_____

_____

_____

Notice your use of closed or open probes.

Coaching Skill: Listen and Respond

You listen and respond to continue dialogue and inspire self-discovery. Your listening encourages your employee or child to reveal his ideas, not only to you, but also to himself. Your responses affirm his ability to choose how he performs. As you guide him toward specific expectations, you willingly give up practices that work for you.

Listening

Listening requires you to devote your full attention to your employee or child, actively following the conversation. Even in the break room or the neighborhood park, focus on what you hear instead of the distractions around you. Sometimes, your mind may wander to irrelevant issues, preventing you from truly hearing. At other times, your mind may race ahead to a blatantly obvious strategy. Effective listening demands energy and commitment both to the person and the process.

> *Years ago, I was conducting a management training seminar about communication skills. The participants were supervisors from local manufacturing plants. As I introduced the topic of active listening, a man spoke up from the back of the room, "Girlie, I don't see what the problem is. I have two ears, you're talking, and we're in the same room. That's all you need to know about listening!"*
>
> —*L.C.D.*

Encourage creative thinking with neutral listening cues such as *Oh? Um . . . . Well . . . . Really? Is that right?* However, certain cues may mistakenly imply that you favor one idea over another, such as when you say *Yes* or *Uh-huh* to indicate *Keep talking.* Ironically, your experience may actually interfere with your ability to coach. Resist the urge to direct or instruct. If you tell your employee or child what to do, you rob him of the satisfaction of determining techniques that work for him.

Rita was driving her thirteen-year-old daughter, Renee, home from school. Renee started telling her mom about her best friend Frannie, who had made rude comments to her throughout the day.

Rita, maternally rising to her daughter's defense, began dispensing advice, "Tomorrow, Renee, when you see Frannie, what you should do is . . . ."

Renee interrupted with, "Mom, I know what to do. I just want to tell you about it."

— C.C.M.

Nonverbal cues such as smiling and nodding let someone know that you want to hear more. Try not to suppress conversation by frowning or shaking your head. Consciously connect through eye contact. When an employee comes into your office, put down whatever you have in your hands and turn from your work to face him. Lean forward to invite further communication. Your young daughter may need to climb on your lap and face you to believe she has your complete attention.

Also pay attention to the nonverbal cues you receive, and respond as if they were spoken. A glare might say *I disagree;* a frown, *I don't understand;* a glance away, *I'm uncomfortable.* However, when an employee fails to return your eye contact, consider that in some cultures looking at you directly would indicate disrespect.

An industrial organization suspected a supervisor of bullying and threatening his employees. I interviewed each employee privately to verify the organization's concerns. After numerous short, uninformative interviews, I encountered Karl, a veteran six months away from retirement. He sat stiffly in his chair and locked his eyes on mine when I asked, "So how are things around here?"

Without looking away, Karl replied deliberately, "Some of the supervisors are real good. They listen to their people and accept their ideas."

As I realized he was hinting at something he was unwilling to say, I responded slowly, "So some of the supervisors don't do that?"

"Yup," he confirmed with a big grin, acknowledging that I had caught on.

"Anything else you want to say?" I asked.

"Nope," Karl answered on his way out the door.

—*L.C.D.*

Responding

As a mentor, you listen to encourage your employee or child to talk and share ideas. You respond to promote deeper insight. Your supportive comments, called *open responses,* invite introspection and clarify confusion. Ultimately, you enable your employee or child to evaluate alternative techniques and determine how they work for her.

Open Responses - Examples

Question	*What will you do if . . . ?*
Statement	*Tell me more about that.*
Reflection	*So, you've already done that.*
Paraphrase	*Let me see if I understand you. You are saying that . . . .*

Used as responses, **questions** draw out relevant details or challenge ideas that seem impractical. *So how would that work when everyone is at lunch?* Or, *What's your plan for getting to your new after-school job?*

Shanice, an MIS manager for a large corporation, presented a troubling request. "Can I fire an employee whose annoying habit repulses me so much that I avoid dealing with him? He clicks his tongue constantly, and I don't even want him around."

Sensing that she had not thought through her emotional reaction, I asked "When the two of you discussed how you feel about his habit, what did he say?"

Her long pause indicated serious consideration. "I have never told him how I feel. If I do, maybe I can help him overcome it."

—*L.C.D.*

Statements used as responses differ from statements about observations and expectations. They summarize your understanding and direct the conversation toward closure. *My understanding is that people on the overtime list will be called first. Then, you'll call the temp agency.* Or, *If I understand you correctly, you're going to ride the number 39 bus to your after-school job, and I will pick you up at five-thirty.*

If your first responsive statement implies strong approval, you limit further creative ideas. Instead of *That's good,* comment on specific parts of the idea that sound feasible. *Your idea about visiting her personally might indeed relieve some of her concerns.* Or, *Delivering your papers before Mass sounds like it would give you the time you need later in the morning.*

Juleen worried about two-and-a-half-year-old Anja's continued use of a bottle. She gently expressed her concern, "You know some children your age don't drink milk out of a bottle. They use a cup. I wonder how you could do that, too."

Anja looked at her intently for a moment and then brightly replied, "I know, Mama. Let's put water in the baba."

Juleen, surprised at how easily Anja had come up with a plan to meet her expectation, said, "Okay. Then we'll put the milk in your cup." Within three days, Anja lost interest in the bottle altogether.

— *C.C.M.*

Reflecting offers a verbal mirror to the employee or child and essentially repeats her words with a different inflection. Your comment does not necessarily mean that you agree but simply that you understand. Your support encourages closure on her personal strategies. Reflecting can sound like a statement or a question. *So you think that you and Sumiko will be good partners on this project.* Or, *You're changing your volunteer time at the pet shelter to Saturday mornings?*

> *Estelle attended a company-wide training seminar for retail super-visors, more to complain aloud than to learn. The group endured her complaints for several hours. Finally, Estelle railed that no one in her office listened to her anymore and that "I constantly have to tell them everything."*
>
> *Penny, another participant at Estelle's table, quietly responded, "You think no one listens to you because you constantly have to tell them everything?"*

—*L.C.D.*

Paraphrasing uses your own words to confirm your understand-ing. Reframe what you hear, asking for verification. *Let me see if I understand you. You are saying you were late today because of the meet-ing last night?* Or, *You don't have homework tonight?*

> *Celeste was concerned about her eight-year-old son, Forrest. In addi-tion to adjusting to a new school, he was frequently teased by his brothers. Forrest often maintained that he was "stupid," although Celeste tried to help him see that everyone makes mistakes.*
>
> *One day when Celeste pulled into a parking lot, the attendant made a rude remark about her driving. Later in the afternoon, Celeste shared the story with Forrest. He listened intently and then commented, "You felt stupid, didn't you, Mom?"*

— *C.C.M.*

Unlike open responses, **closed responses** shut down dialogue. They demean an employee or child with a judgmental or dismissive comment. *I don't think you have the backbone to handle it.* Or, *There's no way you'll be able to save enough money for a car.* Some managers and parents see humor in sarcastic or cutting remarks. *Just call you spineless!* Or, *Well, I'm not making room in the garage anytime soon!* However, shutting down dialogue does not close the subject. Instead, it can provoke the employee or child, intensify the next discussion, and build resentment.

> *Polly came to the counseling office with her fifteen-year-old son, Terry, concerned about his inattention to his schoolwork. Terry began to describe some of the factors that were preventing him from focusing on his work.*
>
> *As I asked questions and listened, I could tell that Terry had, in fact, thought through some of his difficulties and had even considered how he might deal with them. Assuming the supportive role of the coach, I encouraged Terry to pursue some of his ideas. Polly interrupted, "You just wait. You'll see him give up!"*
>
> — *C.C.M.*

At times, however, your employee or child may resist creating new techniques. *I just don't know what to do. Tell me what you think I should do.* Take care as you respond. Giving advice too quickly interrupts the opportunity to develop independent skills. Also beware of an absurd suggestion that attempts to shift responsibility back to you. *You could hire three more people, and that would fix it.* Or, *You could buy me my own car, and then I would get to school on time.* Simply avoid responding at all and ask for another idea.

With very young children, offer concrete suggestions followed by questions. Describe possibilities to initiate ideas, but refrain from making choices for your child. *Sammy is coming to play, so let's think about sharing your toys. If your teddy bear is too special, you could put it away, or you could ask Sammy to bring his teddy bear, or you could decide to play outside instead. What do you want to do?* With encouragement and practice, children can create their own ways to accomplish expected results.

Increase your awareness of various open responses with the following examples and worksheets.

OPEN RESPONSES AT WORK - EXAMPLES

Employee's Comment: *I didn't budget for that.*
Open Response (Question): *How can you adjust the budget?*

Employee's Comment: *I'm going to print the rate card before the brochure.*
Open Response (Statement): *So you will finish the rate card first.*

Employee's Comment: *I guess I could come in this weekend to work on it.*
Open Response (Reflection): *So you could come in this weekend?*

Employee's Comment: *The company's new process won't work in this office.*
Open Response (Paraphrase): *We can't use the new process here?*

OPEN RESPONSES AT HOME - EXAMPLES

Child's Comment: *I've looked everywhere for my brown sweater.*
Open Response (Question): *Where did you last see it?*

Child's Comment: *Everybody in my class hates me.*
Open Response (Statement): *Sounds like you had a rough day at school today.*

Child's Comment: *I want to get some gum when we go to the grocery store.*
Open Response (Reflection): *You'd like to have some gum.*

Child's Comment: *I'm never going back to see that dog next door.*
Open Response (Paraphrase): *You're going to take a break from Blackie?*

OPEN RESPONSES AT WORK - PRACTICE

Increase your skill at making open responses. Complete the first example; then record comments you hear and practice possible responses.

Employee's Comment: *I'll put only experienced people on my team.*

Open Response: _____

_____

_____

Employee's Comment: _____

_____

Open Response: _____

_____

_____

Employee's Comment: _____

_____

Open Response: _____

_____

_____

Employee's Comment: _____

_____

Open Response: _____

_____

_____

OPEN RESPONSES AT HOME - PRACTICE

Increase your skill at making open responses. Complete the first example; then record comments you hear and practice possible responses.

Child's Comment: *While the neighbors are on vacation, I'll just feed their pets every other day.*

Open Response: _____

_____

_____

Child's Comment: _____

_____

Open Response: _____

_____

_____

Child's Comment: _____

_____

Open Response: _____

_____

_____

Child's Comment: _____

_____

Open Response: _____

_____

Connecting the Mentoring Model: Coaching and Structuring

Successful coaching depends on the foundation built by structuring. In the mentoring model the up arrow, on the left side of structuring, represents the transition from structuring to coaching. Through coaching, your employee or child learns how to meet the values and expectations of the organization or family.

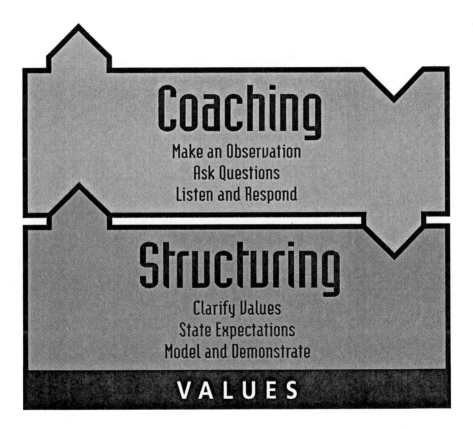

Coaching
Make an Observation
Ask Questions
Listen and Respond

Structuring
Clarify Values
State Expectations
Model and Demonstrate

V A L U E S

You can move up or down the mentoring model because the strategies are interrelated. If your employee's or child's emerging skills do not meet your values or your expectations, return to structuring as illustrated by the down arrow on the right side of the model.

When you restructure for your employee or child, you revisit clarifying values, stating expectations, modeling and demonstrating. After restructuring, return to coaching.

Returning to a former strategy may comprise mere moments within a conversation. Or, it may necessitate numerous discussions that occur over weeks or months until your employee or child proves her readiness to move on. Reverting to a former strategy naturally occurs within the mentoring process and provides opportunity to reevaluate her progress as well as your mentoring skills.

After coaching, your young child or less experienced employee may not meet your expectations perfectly. Restructuring in this instance takes very little time or emphasis. Simply show patience, validate her effort, and remind her of the expectations of the organization or family. When your new assistant handles travel plans for you, your accommodations may not include your preferred king size bed. But she may not have understood that making travel arrangements included meeting personal preferences. When your ten-year-old cleans the kitchen after dinner but fails to wipe the counter, notice what she did right and model wiping the counter tomorrow.

Joyce had talked repeatedly with four-year-old Henry about not hitting other children at childcare. Henry had listened earnestly and participated in the discussion about how he could play with other children without hitting. When he had playmates visit, Joyce observed that Henry was practicing the new techniques they had discussed.

One day Henry's childcare provider mentioned that it had been an unusually rough day among all the children, and even Henry had hit another child. When they got home, Joyce talked for over fifteen minutes about the family's value of respect and expectation of not hitting other children. Henry said very little.

The next time I saw Joyce, she told me her story, "All of my talking about respect and not hitting, and then Henry hit another child! I was so upset that I forgot about how much he has been trying. What I should have said was 'It's hard to learn not to hit, and you are really working at it. Everyone makes mistakes.'"

————————————————————————— *C.C.M.*

At home, you will spend a great deal of time and effort connecting structuring and coaching for your developing child. At times, her misbehavior indicates too much freedom and requires you to restate her limits. When she continually bounces between the dinner table and play, remind her of expected dinner table behavior. However, consider the appropriateness of your expectations for her age or developmental level. A toddler will not sit still for two hours in a gourmet restaurant no matter how much you coach. Avoid putting your child in a situation that she cannot yet handle, and continue to structure.

If you neglect any aspect of structuring, you fail to provide necessary information for your employee or child to succeed. She has difficulty understanding what you expect or appreciating its importance, and you must accept the responsibility for incomplete structuring. Developing a line supervisor's budgeting skills does not help her create a departmental budget if you have not explained the organization's financial goals for the coming year. When you expect your two teenagers to share a car and it does not go well, ask yourself if you have clearly explained your expectations and coached them to work out a schedule for car use.

Wiley, the director of food service at a state maximum-security prison attended my training session on delegating. After the first break he came to me, ashen and most upset. "I called the office to check on things, and I must leave immediately," he told me. "My assistant, Taggart, is filling in for me today—he does that often. He just cancelled the state contract for meat, and ordered meat from his brother-in-law's local meat packing plant."

"He can't do that!" Wiley moaned. "When I left, I told Taggart he was in charge and asked if he had any questions. We talked about how he would put together the work schedule and purchase fresh vegetables, but I never thought to tell him that he couldn't cancel state purchase orders!"

—*L.C.D.*

At work, restructuring becomes more serious when an employee knowingly violates a value of the organization. This may signal an employee's inability to adapt to organizational beliefs. In this instance, each time you restructure, your expectations narrow her choices until she develops appropriate skills or proves unfit for the job.

Teamwork was very important to Heidi, the manager of a major car rental location. She had promoted team projects and problem solving for years, especially among her senior managers. When her operations manager retired, Heidi hired Kenneth from a similar position in another state. He had management experience and maturity–a perfect fit, she thought. She explained the importance of teamwork to Kenneth, and that she expected him to participate on several teams. He assured her that he worked well on teams.

However, after several team meetings, Heidi heard complaints about Kenneth throughout the organization. "He won't listen to anyone's suggestions. He 'pulls rank' constantly by saying that he's the operations manager and we're going to do things his way," reported several managers and a few employees.

Heidi restructured for him. "Kenneth, I may not have been clear enough or emphatic enough about our value of teamwork or the importance of your participation on our teams. This means that you must seriously consider the ideas of others and accept the consensus of the team after their deliberation."

"But I've got so much more experience than most of them," Kenneth began.

"That's true," Heidi interrupted, "but they won't ever get experience if we don't let them. From now on, you must work cooperatively with each team. Now, let's discuss how you might do that. How can you respond to ideas you don't like? I'll be glad to role play with you . . . ."

—*L.C.D.*

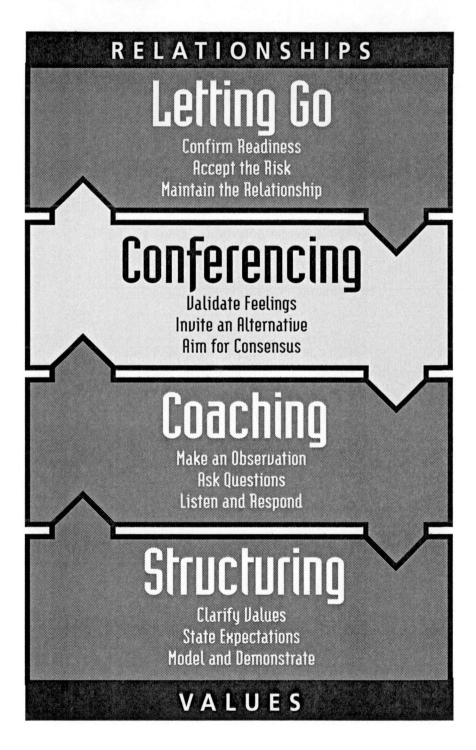

RELATIONSHIPS

Letting Go

Confirm Readiness
Accept the Risk
Maintain the Relationship

Conferencing

Validate Feelings
Invite an Alternative
Aim for Consensus

Coaching

Make an Observation
Ask Questions
Listen and Respond

Structuring

Clarify Values
State Expectations
Model and Demonstrate

VALUES

CHAPTER FOUR

Conferencing

Through **conferencing**, the mentor works together with the employee or child to redefine **what** new expectations fulfill the values of the organization or family. When he masters relevant skills, your focus shifts from encouraging skill development to collaborating to expand expectations. You hold steadfast to values that offer the **why** for behavior. Your employee or child now has complete control of **how** he performs to meet new expectations.

YOUR CONFERENCING SCORE

Items seven through nine on the self-tests in Chapter One indicate your approach to conferencing. Transfer your answers from those items to the box on the next page. Add your scores vertically. Compare your conferencing scores to the descriptions of the four conferencing styles that follow.

Items Related to Conferencing

SELF-TEST FOR WORK

7.	c ____	b ____	d ____	a ____
8.	d ____	c ____	b ____	a ____
9.	d ____	b ____	a ____	c ____
TOTALS	____	____	____	____
	BOSS	MANIPULATOR	MARTYR	MENTOR

SELF-TEST FOR HOME

7.	c ____	b ____	d ____	a ____
8.	d ____	c ____	b ____	a ____
9.	d ____	b ____	a ____	c ____
TOTALS	____	____	____	____
	BOSS	MANIPULATOR	MARTYR	MENTOR

HOW EACH STYLE CONFERENCES

The **boss** does not initiate conferences. He does not entertain the notion that expectations could expand. Nor does he imagine that employees or children could share his responsibility for defining appropriate behavior. The boss does not recognize their readiness or potential to contribute original ideas. In fact, as they mature he finds them more difficult to control. The boss views the personal feelings of others as pointless, their need for change as insubordinate, and collaborative discussion as irrelevant and unproductive. Confronted by emotion, the boss hardens his position even more. The boss manager laments *The more training these people get, the more trouble they are. Why won't they just do what I say?* The boss parent directs *I don't want to hear your excuses. Get back in there and play football.* The demeaning style of the boss provokes and builds resentment.

The **manipulator** feels uneasy about conferencing. Even though she believes in the potential of employees and children, she worries that their increasing capability will make it more difficult to influence what they do. The manipulator reacts to their feelings by offering rewards or threatening punishments. Mistakenly she believes that her external rewards motivate, unaware that participation in conferencing by itself contributes to ownership and internal motivation. When employees suggest changes, the manipulator manager wonders how she will continue to motivate them. *Why do you want to move to that department? Your bonuses will not be as big.* The manipulator parent listens only to discover what will motivate the child. *We can't let you stay out any later. How about if I pay for your pizza instead?*

The **martyr** responds to the feelings of his employees and children by giving in, even if their suggestions violate values. Thus, he prematurely transfers control for behavior, regardless of readiness. Hoping to avoid tension when an employee complains, the martyr manager quickly agrees with her perspective without discussion. *Okay, if you don't want to come to staff meeting, you don't have to.* The martyr parent often defers to his child in an effort to avoid a potential conflict. *Hana just doesn't like to help around the house, so we don't ask her to.*

The **mentor** conferences with employees and children to expand expectations and encourage self-direction. When a mentor recognizes frustration, she listens with care, validates feelings, and willingly discusses suggestions. The mentor manager aims for a resolution that will support an employee's concerns and also accomplish the goals of the organization. *I understand how you feel about not being informed when board decisions affect your job. Communication is* *vital to our work. Let's try your idea of my e-mailing the board meeting minutes to you after each meeting.* The mentor parent recognizes when her maturing child tells her, verbally or nonverbally, that he can help define appropriate behavior. The two-year-old who balks when put in a car seat may simply need to climb in by himself.

CONFERENCING AS A STRATEGY

The mentor initiates a conference when his employee or child signifies that an established expectation feels too restrictive or controlling. Perhaps she carefully avoids an essential task, pushes back with emotion, appears unchallenged, or indicates in some way *This is not working for me.* Even though the employee or child still respects the values of the organization or family and demonstrates necessary skills, she objects to prescribed expectations. Recognizing her experience or maturity, the mentor responds by conferencing. *I hear your concern. Let's sit down and talk about it.* He knows that participation will inspire her internal motivation and encourage her cooperation.

> *Andy, a senior manager I met at a civic meeting, asked to meet me to discuss a problem. When we met for breakfast, he lowered his voice secretively. "What does it mean to col-lab-or-ate?" he sounded out.*
>
> *I explained that it means to work closely with others to solve problems and asked what caused his interest. Andy explained, "I have a new financial officer who keeps telling me that I talk too much at staff meetings, and I need to collaborate more. I don't know what she wants me to do."*
>
> *For the next few months, we met weekly for breakfast and discussed questions he could ask his staff about their concerns. Andy reported each week and was invigorated by what he learned. Our breakfasts ended the day Andy's financial officer told him he was becoming a much better collaborator.*
>
> —*L.C.D.*

The mentor collaborates to redefine, in innovative terms, the very notion of appropriateness. He broadens expectations to allow more interpretation by the employee or child. After a conference with a traveling saleswoman, *Employees must dress professionally at all times* may become *Employees should dress appropriately for customer contact.* As a father conferences with his ten-year-old son about bedtime, they may change *Lights out at eight-thirty* to *After you go to bed at eight-thirty, you may read for a while. Just turn out the light when you are finished.* Conferencing conversations result in new, mutually acceptable expectations. As the mentor moves beyond control, he realizes that most expectations can expand.

> *Hunter and Imma were distressed that three-year-old Taylor would not wash his hands. Even though they insisted that he wash before meals, after using the toilet, and after playing in the dirt, he still cried and fought when it was hand-washing time. Finally, they acknowledged, "Taylor, you really have strong feelings about not washing your hands."*
>
> *"Yeah," he sniffed. "It makes my thumb taste like soap."*
>
> *"Oh!" replied Hunter and Imma together, "when you suck your thumb you don't like the taste of the soap, so that makes you not want to wash your hands." Taylor was visibly relieved that his parents understood. As they discussed the issue, all three agreed on a new expectation: when Taylor washes his hands, he no longer needs to use soap on his thumb.*
>
> —————————————————————————————— *C.C.M.*

At work, the mentor manager constantly looks for ways to empower his employee and enhance her contributions. *Frieda, you seem to be interested in extending your loan authority. Tell me more about what you have in mind.* The manager respectfully accepts his employee's feelings. Even when she misunderstands, he stifles his impulse to argue. *I can understand how you might believe your current loan limit restricts your ability to respond quickly to your customers. That could be frustrating.* The mentor eagerly welcomes a variety of ideas without feeling threatened or believing that he must champion tradition. He aims for consensus about an outcome that accomplishes the organization's goals. *An increased loan limit would position you to make some commercial loans. Would you be willing to go to classes to learn about commercial loans?* The mentor arranges to check back with his employee to evaluate the new expectation. *Let's get together again next month after you finish the classes.*

Katrina is the director of a large, nationally accredited childcare center. One of her primary expectations is that each classroom will have an indoor sandbox. One day after work, Margaret, the prekindergarten teacher, stopped by Katrina's office.

"Can I talk with you about a boy in my class?" Margaret began.

"You sound concerned, Margaret. What is the situation?"

"Clayton will be going to kindergarten in the fall," Margaret explained. "Yet, every day he goes straight to the sandbox to play. He just loves it, but I am concerned that he may not be developing enough other interests for school."

"Hmmm. What ideas do you have?"

"I was thinking that if we could close the sandbox for a few days then I could observe what else Clayton can do and what other activities he might like."

"You know I believe that young children need to play in the sand. But if Clayton really needs to play to this extent, he may not be ready for kindergarten. I can see how closing the sandbox might help you evaluate him. Try it tomorrow and let me know what happens."

—*L.C.D.*

At home, a child wants her parents to listen and to understand her point of view. When she resists an expectation, her parent must take the time to conference. Often, parents simply want to enforce existing expectations. Yet, repeating *Turn off that CD player* night after night builds frustration and resentment. Instead, a mentor parent initiates a conference by validating her feelings. *I know you want to play your CDs late at night.* Hearing the child's perspective gains additional information. *I understand that you enjoy music while you study.* By identifying his own key issues, the mentor helps her consider both sides of the situation. *When I hear the loud bass through the walls, it keeps me awake.* Aiming for consensus often results in a new, mutually acceptable expectation. *I like your suggestion of turning down the bass. Let's try that tonight and see how it goes.* Conferencing offers more satisfactory solutions than repeated nagging.

> *Owen and Colleen were exhausted with seven-year-old Kari, who was getting up numerous times during the night wanting to be with her parents. Owen and Colleen just wanted to be together in their own bed and enjoy a good night's sleep. They had tried ignoring her, reprimanding her, and even sleeping in her room. Nothing worked. When they conferenced with Kari, she insisted, "Sometimes, I just need to be near you."*
>
> *Owen and Colleen shared that they could remember how it felt to be alone at night when they were children. They all talked about ways Kari could feel comfortable and everyone in the family could still get a good night's sleep. All three agreed to keep a sleeping bag on the floor by the parents' bed so that Kari could quietly come in and sleep near them when she felt lonely.*
>
> — *C.C.M.*

The employee or child may speak candidly if she believes in the mentor's trustworthiness and willingness to listen. An employee may explain *I don't want to submit a budget until I get the final numbers from Personnel.* A child may maintain *I have play practice every night this week, so my room will be a mess. But I plan to clean it on Saturday.*

Without such candor, the mentor must watch for verbal or non-verbal clues that suggest a need to conference. The employee or child may appear bored, uninterested, or unchallenged. Most commonly, she seems reluctant to do what the mentor expects. An employee misses a deadline, drags her feet, or cannot seem to complete a project. *My budget is not finished. It has been so busy around here.* Similarly, a child "forgets," gets distracted, or makes excuses. *I didn't have time to clean my room. I'll do it tomorrow.*

When the employee or child emotionally rejects the expectation, the mentor recognizes an opportunity to conference. The employee may pick a rule to pieces, argue over each step, or generally push back. *I don't see why I have to put a preliminary budget together. Accounting is just going to tear it apart.* A child often indicates the need for conferencing by pouting, crying, or raging. *Your clean room rule is stupid. You don't even understand what all I have to do!* A mentor must continually attend to the relationship, even in the midst of disagreement.

> *Mozelle could tell that her data entry employees were not happy. They complained about their work assignments, pushed the limit with breaks and days off, and continually sniped at each other. Concerned, she asked each employee to list three most and least favorite tasks in the office.*
>
> *Her follow-up conferences uncovered issues Mozelle had not previously suspected. Some people disliked their currently assigned tasks; others were simply bored. Most everyone expressed an interest in learning more. Based on their discussions, Mozelle reassigned tasks and allowed time for employees to train each other. The group developed a rotation plan to exchange tasks regularly.*
>
> *Mozelle continued to require certain skill competencies but primarily focused on final results. Morale, attendance, and cooperation improved almost immediately.*
>
> —*L.C.D.*

A new or unusual occurrence also calls for a conference. A manager can enlist cooperation for a major project with *The accreditation team's report suggests several changes in your department. How do you suggest we implement them?* A parent may conference with a teenager to solve a problem. *My car is in the shop tomorrow, so I will need a ride to work. What are your car needs before school?*

Sometimes, the mentor observes that an employee or child has the skill or maturity to take on a new challenge. Through conferencing, a manager can elicit both commitment to a new assignment and feelings about it. *The merger will impact your department. I'd like for you to be in charge of the project.* A parent might initiate a conference with *Now that you are eighteen, we need to talk about getting your own checking account.*

Toni, the coordinator of training programs for a small service organization was asked to administer several weekend training sessions as a result of staffing changes. Sensing her animosity one Monday, Clovis, her manager, called her to his office.

"Toni, you seem tired and out of sorts. I'm worried about you."

"Oh, I'm okay, Clovis," she sighed. "I'm just really worn-out after working this weekend. I know you want me here every day, but it'll be twelve days straight before I get a break, and I'm going to have to work every night just to get caught up on my chores at home."

"Working the weekends without a break is a real hardship for you."

"Oh, I can do it, but it is difficult. If I could only have the following Monday and Tuesday at home it would sure help."

"I can understand that. Let me check on our comp time policy and get back to you. If we can't let you off both days, would one day work?"

—*L.C.D.*

Conferencing symbolizes growth for everyone involved. For the employee or child, it signifies trust and respect from someone who takes her concerns seriously. For the manager or parent, the conferencing experience stretches his ability to appreciate alternatives. As he listens to the feelings of the employee or child, he confronts the possibility that more than one course of action will support the values of his organization or family.

Conferencing at Work

The real or perceived power that accompanies a management position sometimes intimidates an employee or inflates a manager's image. As a result, the manager's requests for suggestions or ideas may yield few responses until he proves his willingness to listen and implement agreed-upon changes. Employees almost always have recommendations; past experience with a manager guides their decision to voice them.

> *Jack, a radio station manager, asked me to come make his staff "talk in staff meetings again." I asked how long it had been since they talked openly and what had caused the change.*
>
> *"It was several months ago," Jack explained. "During a meeting, I asked for their concerns about the way keys to various doors were distributed and, man, did they have ideas and strong feelings. At the end of their discussion, I passed around the new key distribution policy I had written before the meeting. And, you know, they haven't spoken up about anything else since then."*
>
> —*L.C.D.*

Conferencing with an employee pushes the mentor manager one more step beyond control. When he encourages an employee to become more involved, he must begin with sincere interest in the potential contribution she will make. Consideration of her ideas, as well as his own, should contribute to a partnership endeavor. Conferencing requires his saying *Let's consider new ideas together* not *Bring your ideas for my approval.*

Conferencing At Home

A very young child tends to express her dissatisfaction physically: throwing herself on the floor, hitting a friend, or taking a toy. If, as a mentor, you have previously structured and coached about her behavior, conferencing now becomes an appropriate strategy. Yet, the child's lack of language or verbal skills makes it difficult to articulate what is not working for her.

> *Hillary and her daughter, four-year-old Lexi, were having a disagreement. They decided to each take time in their rooms to cool down so that they could later resume their discussion in a more respectful way. When they got back together, Hillary was still frustrated, "Lexi, you shouldn't have said . . . ."*
>
> *Lexi, hands on hips, replied, "Mom, I am only four years old, and I didn't know the right words."*
>
> — *C.C.M.*

As the child matures, her language capabilities increase, but she does not know that language can solve problems unless her parent shows her. She may still respond physically by poking a sibling or slamming a door. Through conferencing, the mentor parent models the use of language to express feelings. He encourages the child's potential to see the perspective of another person, expands her understanding of alternative solutions, and builds her ability to collaborate. Without parental intervention, the child may not have the opportunity to learn these skills.

Annie had invited three-year-old Jeremy over for the morning to play with her son Gabe. Before long Jeremy came to Annie, complaining that Gabe would not share the building blocks.

Annie asked, "Jeremy, what do you do at home when you have a problem?"

Jeremy confidently answered, "When I have a problem, I tell my mom, and she solves it!"

—————————————————————————————— *C.C.M.*

CONFERENCING SKILLS

The conferencing strategy shifts your emphasis from coaching based on established expectations to collaborating with employees and children to expand those expectations. As a mentor, you conference when you practice the following three skills.

Conferencing
Validate Feelings
Invite an Alternative
Aim for Consensus

Conferencing Skill: Validate Feelings

Your employees and children share universal feelings. Try to understand the emotion embedded in their words and behavior. Without judging, describe and accept the underlying feeling. Employees can feel stressed, furious, appreciative, confused, frustrated, or frazzled. Children experience anger, joy, contentment, pride, jealousy, or disappointment. Expand your awareness of a wide range of feelings, such as peaceful, perplexed, concerned, worried, scared, safe, resentful, provoked, or revengeful.

Your own emotions often make it difficult to deal with the emotions of your employee or child. Yet, the success of your conference depends on your commitment to focus on his emotions and ideas rather than your own. In order to understand his perspective, restrain your feelings about what seems appropriate to you. The employee or child must trust that you care about his feelings and that you will listen respectfully to his thoughts. Without that trust, he may not tell you what he really thinks. The employee may contend *Nothing's bothering me. It's okay,* while to himself he says *You wouldn't understand.* The child may huff, *Dad, you just don't get it!*

Laureen, a manufacturing plant Human Resources director, called me with an unusual request for training. "Can you do a short training session on Humor in the Workplace for our secretaries during a brown bag lunch?"

"You mean with a clown nose and a 'fright wig?" I asked jokingly.

"Exactly! They all seem so depressed lately. We think something fun will cheer them up," Laureen explained. I asked what had happened lately to upset them and learned that a month earlier there had been sixteen secretaries, and now only eight remained after a plant-wide layoff.

"How do these eight feel about doubling their work?" I questioned.

"Oh, we didn't ask them," Laureen responded. "We just told them that they had to pick up all the slack."

—L.C.D.

145

As you conference, accept the uniqueness of your employee or child and realize that his perceptions reflect his reality. An employee may object that *Making me drive all the way back to the office just to sign out is ridiculous.* Your child may protest that *Vegetables are disgusting, and I'm not going to eat them.* When you respond, validate feelings in order to establish an open climate for self-disclosure. To your employee, you may respond *Having to make that long drive back is frustrating.* To your child, you might confirm *You really have strong feelings about those vegetables.*

When an employee or child feels understood, he will freely express his concerns. This is a fragile moment. *I really resent not being paid for my mileage.* Or, *Corn on the cob is too messy. It drips everywhere.* Once he trusts you enough to risk vulnerability, you must support his disclosure of feelings whether or not you agree. *It sounds like your frustration is with our travel policy* or *It feels yucky to have butter dripping all over.* Disregarding his feelings diminishes his trust. *That's not such a big deal. Don't complain.* Or, *Quit crying. Get over it.*

Three-year-old Alex refused to sleep in his room, convinced that a rhinoceros lived there. His mother, Jenn, appealed to his intellect, showing him in books that a rhinoceros could not possibly live in their community. After I suggested that she enter into his reality, Jenn told Alex, "I've been thinking about the rhinoceros in your room. What do you think we should do about it?"

Visibly relieved that at last his mother recognized the danger they were in, he sighed, "I don't know, Mom. What should we do?"

Jenn shared, "I've been thinking about the neighbor's goat pen down the road. Do you think we could get him to stay there?"

"Yeah," Alex replied. "We could keep him down there. But how are we going to get him there?"

"Hmmmm," Jenn mused. "We'll have to think about that. I wonder how we could get a rhinoceros to walk from our house down the road?"

"Oh! I've got a good idea for that!" Alex exclaimed. Alex ran and got a dog leash for the rhinoceros and marched into his room. He and Jenn dragged the dog leash to the neighbor's goat pen, put the rhinoceros inside, and happily went home. Alex slept peacefully in his room all night long.

— *C.C.M.*

As you conference, listen to the actual words and also attend to nonverbal cues. They will help you understand underlying feelings. Ask yourself the following questions.

Understanding Feelings

1. **What is the employee or child *saying*?**

2. **What is the employee or child *doing*?**

3. **What is the employee or child *feeling*?**

1. What is the employee or child saying?

As you listen to employees' feelings, consider both their words and the context. People like to talk about what they do and how they work. When a manager takes time to ask an employee's opinion or ideas, most employees consider it a compliment. If an employee trusts that a manager sincerely wants to listen, he usually will take advantage of the chance to be heard.

Geoffrey, president of a large midwestern advertising agency, expressed no interest in his monthly meetings with small groups of employees. "The original idea was for them to get to know me and for us to talk about the future of the agency," he explained. "But they only want to talk about more parking places, free cokes in the break room, and better desk chairs. I want to talk about market share, ad rates, and profit margins. I'm ready to cancel the meetings."

I asked Geoffrey if he could imagine that the employees might have something they wanted to tell him at these meetings. He replied, "But I don't really care what they have to say." Sadly, at that point, I agreed with him, given his unwillingness to listen to his employees' concerns and feelings.

—*L.C.D.*

In less trusting environments, employees notice others within earshot and consciously weigh the politics of their comments. An employee who publicly says *Our team enjoys working together* may describe different feelings in private. Employees can play games with their words, hiding how they feel. Skillfully subtle, they may argue or overexplain. Talking about feelings makes some employees uncomfortable because they want to avoid an excitable or impulsive image. They may not admit, even to themselves, what they feel. *It's fine with me. Really.*

On the other hand, children talk about their feelings quite candidly. In an emotional situation, the child's words generally contain his complete truth. Often, he describes his position exactly. Yet, parents may easily discount his feelings because of their own needs, interests, or motivations. When your daughter says, *I don't want to go to school tomorrow,* take the time to find out her meaning. Instead of reacting with *You have to go to school. I can't stay home with you,* stop and intently listen to the child's exact words. *You seem really concerned about school tomorrow.* Validating her feelings will encourage her to share more.

Coming home from their family vacation, six-year-old Nathaniel "had a huge fit in the car most of the way home," his mother told me. I asked her what Nathaniel said was wrong.

Jane replied, "He kept yelling that I didn't pay attention to him while we were on vacation. He said that I just talked to Sharon all the time.

Sharon is my friend whose family went with us. But that doesn't make sense because I was available to Nathaniel the whole time."

Soon, Jane realized that Nathaniel's words were in fact his truth. Even though she was available, his perception was that she had not initiated special times just with him.

—— C.C.M.

2. What is the employee or child doing?

Nonverbal cues often provide the clearest understanding of feelings. When an employee slams her purse on the desk and yanks her chair out, she screams nonverbally. Another employee who avoids you in the hall and does not return your calls sends a more subtle nonverbal message. An employee's tone of voice, look, or eye contact all communicate feelings. React to nonverbal cues as though spoken. *I can see that you are upset. What's up?*

Yolanda had recently moved from an administrative assistant position to the front desk of the law office. She agreed to the move at the time, in fact expressing relief at the reduction in her paperwork. After the first week, she began to take longer and longer breaks. Soon, she turned her desk and chair to face away from the entrance. This made visitors have to step completely around her desk to make eye contact with her. Casey, her supervisor, asked her regularly how she liked the new job, and her standard reply was, "It's okay."

Finally, Casey sat down beside her late one afternoon and said, "Sometimes, a job just doesn't turn out to be what you thought it would."

Yolanda burst into tears and told Casey, "I get so frustrated with the people who constantly come in and interrupt me. I tried moving my desk, but it still didn't help."

—L.C.D.

Because of a very young child's limited language, insight into his feelings comes more directly from his behavior. His tantrum says *Something is not right.* As you try to interpret his feelings, give him words to use in the future. *You are frustrated because you were playing with that bear, and Tony took it away from you.* As your child grows, continue to teach him how to tell, rather than show, his feelings.

> *Three-year-old Cameron struggled with his mother over wearing his raincoat. Each day that it rained, Paige recited her list of reasons why a raincoat was necessary. "Cameron, you have to wear your raincoat so that your clothes won't get wet when you play outside at preschool. All the other children will be wearing their raincoats, and your teacher expects you to wear yours."*
>
> *The more Paige explained, the more Cameron fought and tried to run away. Finally, after many difficult days, Paige looked at him caringly and reflected, "You really hate this raincoat, don't you?"*
>
> *Cameron stopped crying, looked her in the eyes, and said, "Yes." Realizing that his mom at last understood, Cameron put on his raincoat and walked out the door to go to preschool.*
>
> — *C.C.M.*

3. What is the employee or child feeling?

When your employee or child trusts you, he willingly shares his feelings. Your employee says to you *I refunded Mrs. Campbell's money, but I really think she broke that mixer herself. I don't like having to refund money when I think someone is just trying to get something for nothing.* Your child may confide in you *Mrs. Arastu made the whole class stay after school just because of two kids. I just hate that teacher!* When he candidly vents to you, you do not need to argue, explain, or convince him of the validity of your expectation. He primarily wants you to hear and understand him. You respond to your employee: *Sounds like you're frustrated with our return policy. I can tell you feel strongly about returning money to someone whom you think is dishonest.* To your child you might say *You must have had a rough day.*

Your awareness of an employee's work issues enhances your understanding of his feelings. Knowing that a new employee recently created her first window display allows you to confirm her feeling of pride. Realizing that an employee's computer malfunctioned allows you to read his emotion as exasperation with equipment rather than with you. Recognizing the surrounding circumstances helps you to describe emotion more accurately and to place it in an appropriate context.

Patrick, president of a small-town bank, was perplexed. "We have always expected our officers to call on customers, but these new officers just won't do it. I really don't know why. I spend time with them every month, sharing all our financial information so that they can talk knowledgeably about the bank when they visit."

I suggested that he sit down with several of the officers he knew well and ask why they thought the officers were hesitant. When I saw him next, he was quick to tell me that he had discovered the reason for the officers' reluctance. "They're scared of what they might be asked," he said. "And I think I'm the reason they are. They said all my data made them think they had to make formal presentations when they visited."

Patrick apologized at the next meeting. "I asked what would be more helpful to prepare them for visits and acknowledged that I still get nervous sometimes before a visit. They talked a lot about what they dreaded, and we are even role playing now when we meet. They're making visits and reporting on them at our meetings, too."

—*L.C.D.*

Your young child's repertoire of feelings will include *happy* and *mad.* As you help him to develop his emotional intelligence, you expand his ability to discern feelings. When he feels *happy,* he can learn to use words like *satisfied, pleased,* or *excited. Mad* feelings may now become *confused, frustrated,* or *furious.* Attending to his emotional development enhances your relationship. You will find that he no longer automatically responds with an angry temper but can describe what he truly feels.

> *Peyton noticed his five-year-old son, Jareth, moping about the house. Peyton tried to help Jareth identify his feeling, "You seem sad."*
>
> *Jareth answered, "I hate my life. I want to die."*
>
> *Peyton worried how he should respond to such serious emotion. "Sounds like you have some really strong feelings inside, Jareth."*
>
> *"Yes," Jareth sighed. "I'm bored." Peyton was relieved to know that Jareth was just bored. This was a feeling he could handle.*
>
> —*C.C.M.*

The following examples and worksheets will guide your practice validating feelings.

VALIDATING FEELINGS - EXAMPLES

You seem . . .

> . . . disappointed that the seminar was cancelled.
>
> . . . anxious about making your speech for class president.

It must have been . . .

> . . . unnerving when the truck overturned.
>
> . . . embarrassing when you fell down and skinned your knee
> on the playground.

That must have . . .

> . . . confused you when the system wouldn't take your password.
>
> . . . surprised you when that big dog ran around the corner of the house.

You must be . . .

> . . . hurt by the team's decision.
>
> . . . afraid that I will be disappointed in your report card.

If I were you, I would feel . . .

> . . . frustrated that my insurance claim has not been processed.
>
> . . . lonely since Reanna moved out of the neighborhood.

I can tell you have strong feelings about . . .

> . . . the new computer system.
>
> . . . my calling you on the cell phone when you were on your date
> with Michael.

It sounds like _____ is really important to you.

> . . . changing your schedule . . .
>
> . . . going to Samantha's birthday party . . .

VALIDATING FEELINGS - PRACTICE

AT WORK

Describe recent situations when your employee expressed feelings about an existing expectation.

1. _____
_____
_____

2. _____
_____
_____

AT HOME

Describe recent situations when your child expressed feelings about an existing expectation.

1. _____
_____
_____

2. _____
_____
_____

Now try the starters on the following page to practice validating feelings.

VALIDATING FEELINGS - PRACTICE

You seem . . .

    Manager: _____

    Parent: _____

It must have been . . .

    Manager: _____

    Parent: _____

That must have . . .

    Manager: _____

    Parent: _____

You must be . . .

    Manager: _____

    Parent: _____

If I were you, I would feel . . .

    Manager: _____

    Parent: _____

I can tell you have strong feelings about . . .

    Manager: _____

    Parent: _____

It sounds like _____ is really important to you.

    Manager: _____

    Parent: _____

Conferencing Skill: Invite an Alternative

Even when you validate the feelings of your employee or child, she still may choose not to comply with an expectation that she finds too restrictive. For example, your employee may retort *I still feel that my workload makes me work harder than anyone else around here.* Likewise, your daughter may argue *I told you I won't go to bed because I'm afraid of the monster under my bed.* You may wish to respond by dismissing, arguing, or demanding. *You don't work any harder than anyone else around here. It's your attitude that is the problem.* Or, *There's no such thing as monsters. Go to bed.* However, such closed responses disregard the employee's or child's right to an opinion and shut down dialogue.

> *Regina told me of her frustration with her thirteen-year-old son Terence when he came home from school each day. "I expect him to come straight home from school and take the dog for a walk for forty-five minutes. He and I fight about it every day." I asked Regina if she had conferenced with Terence to seek other ideas for exercising the dog.*
>
> *"Why?" she asked. "Somebody has to walk the dog, and I don't want to do it!"*
>
> — *C.C.M.*

After you recognize and put aside your need to control behavior, invite suggestions for broadening the current expectation. Your employee must envision a way to reduce her workload or simplify her duties. *What is it that causes you to think that? What could we do to change it?* Your child needs to think about changing her bedtime routine to help her feel safe. *How can we take care of that monster so that you can sleep in your bed?*

> *Helen, an elementary school teacher, liked to come home from work each day and tidy the house before she prepared dinner for the family. She expected that nine-year-old Kendee would help by unloading the*

dishwasher. However, Kendee often complained, "I hate unloading the dishwasher."

Finally, Helen sat down with Kendee and validated her feelings. "Unloading the dishwasher really seems to bother you."

Kendee replied, "Mom, I know it is important that everyone help around the house, but I just don't like to come home from school and do the same thing every day."

As Helen listened, she realized that Kendee was not trying to argue but was frankly disclosing her feelings. As they conferenced, Helen asked, "If you don't like to unload the dishwasher, what would you like to do to help?"

Kendee answered, "How would it work if each day you ask me to help with something that you need?"

Although initially Helen was uncomfortable with the thought of not having a set routine, she accepted Kendee's proposal. Before long, Helen really liked the new system. In fact, she enjoyed having an all-purpose helper.

—*C.C.M.*

Considering a novel suggestion that seems contrary to your own expectation requires open-mindedness and self-restraint. When you hear *I want to change my schedule to thirty-five hours a week* or *I want you to stand guard in my room all night,* you may feel a loss of control because of your comfort with past practice. However, when you conference, your attitude should reflect a willingness to hear options that could work.

Marsh, a successful broadcast network executive, confounded his employees with his desk plaque that read "Only Bring Me Solutions." When an employee began describing all the difficulties with a procedure or an assignment, Marsh would listen completely and then ask, "What do you suggest we do about it?"

Those who had come expecting Marsh to correct the situation were sent away because they had not considered themselves to be part of the solution. He welcomed them when they could contribute their own suggestions.

—*L.C.D.*

Explain any applicable boundaries. The employee or child may not consider restraints of time, money, policies and procedures, impact on other individuals, or the burden to the organization or family. *Changing your schedule to thirty-five hours a week would eliminate your health benefits.* Or, *I can't stand guard in your room all night long because I need to sleep, too.* Different from closed responses, boundaries explain facts to consider before modifying an existing expectation.

When you think of boundaries, your immediate response may reflect a personal preference rather than a legitimate restriction rooted in values. *It's too expensive* may really mean *I don't want to look at the budget again.* Or, *I can't do it* may serve as an excuse for *I don't want to be inconvenienced.* Challenge the boundaries you describe to make certain they truly exist.

Several elementary school teachers had come to their principal, Pauletta, about the school's Halloween observances. Some were concerned about the cost of costumes, and others asked about children with certain religious beliefs. Pauletta started to create a policy, then recognized an opportunity to invite alternatives from the teachers. She asked for a team of volunteers to design the celebration and shared the following boundaries with them.

Please answer this question:
How can we recognize and celebrate October 31 in a manner permitting participation by all our students?

Our plan should reflect these school values:
Respect for all beliefs.

Sensitivity to the economic levels of our families.

Let's get together for our first meeting in mid-September.

As a result of their planning, everyone at the school enjoyed that year's Fall Festival!

—L.C.D.

Once you understand the concern of your employee or child and she understands relevant boundaries, her suggestion may offer an obvious choice. Recognize its validity, and accept the possibility of adopting her alternative. *Okay, we'll try letting the answering service pick up on calls during the noon hour and early afternoon and see if that gives you more time at your desk.* Or, *Let's try that! Your toy broom should get that monster out from under your bed.*

However, when your experience suggests possible pitfalls, help your employee or child anticipate them. *So how would that work on Tuesdays when we have staff meetings at noon?* Or, *How will you reach all the way under your bed with your toy broom?* Yet, if she insists on her plan, realize that valuable lessons come through experience with failure. If her suggestion meets your values, have the courage to risk trying something new, even if it makes you uncomfortable. If it fails, allow her to revise it. More realistic options will become evident after the first . . . and second . . . revision.

"Jessica is a good nurse manager, but she micromanages and makes all the decisions for her people," the hospital administrator told me. "I'll support whatever it takes to help her." I agreed to help her develop less controlling strategies and learn to ask for input from her nurses.

In our first meeting, we struggled to identify even one issue for which Jessica was willing to solicit ideas. Finally, we identified a situation she had decided to resolve by herself. Every morning after the seven o'clock shift change meeting, her sixteen nurses usually crowded around the small medication cart from the Pharmacy Department to gather medications for their assigned patients. Some of the nurses had discovered that they could drink one more cup of coffee if they "waited for the crowd to clear around the cart." Jessica was prepared to dictate rules such as No second cup of coffee *and* Line up to select meds. *As we talked, I focused her on the impact of the nurses' performance, which ultimately she recognized as a basic hospital value: timely treatment.*

At the next staff meeting, without mentioning the cart, Jessica asked how they could guarantee timely medication delivery. After much shuffling and lack of eye contact, one nurse said sarcastically, "Well, we all could come in thirty minutes early. That would give us time." They expected Jessica to reject such an absurd idea and to impose a procedure.

However, as we had agreed, she replied, "Let's try your suggestion for a week and see if we can deliver the meds faster." Soon after the meeting, nurses began to ask Jessica to reconsider, thinking of baby-sitters, car pools, and family routines. Yet, her predetermined response was, "It's what you came up with. Let's give your idea a fair try for a week." Throughout the week, she resisted her urge to fix their solution or impose one of her own, while I dealt with the hospital administrator's concern about overtime costs.

At the following week's staff meeting, Jessica complimented the nurses on their timely treatment during the past week. Then, she asked them to evaluate their plan and offer other alternatives. Believing now that their ideas would be implemented, they created a new procedure that did work for them—including a second medication cart!

—*L.C.D.*

Young children do not have a great deal of experience thinking of options for behavior. With your young child, you must model the process of considering alternatives. As she matures and you invite her to solve problems in more complex situations, she will gain confidence and experience. Your child will surprise you at how quickly she catches on to this process. Encourage her independent thought, and have patience as she develops her ability to verbalize feelings and generate alternative solutions.

Four-year-old Dallas was weary of spending time at the doctor's office with his mom, Nola, and his new baby brother. One morning Nola awakened him with news of another appointment that morning. Dallas cried, "I don't want to go back to that doctor's office!"

Nola empathized, "I know you are tired of going there so much, but I can't leave you at home by yourself."

Dallas brightened and replied, "We could call my baby-sitter."

"Okay," Nola responded. "Here's the phone. Her number is 555-9707."

Dallas got his baby-sitter on the line and had a short conversation. Hanging up, he looked despondent. "She can't come."

"Oh, that's unfortunate. I wonder what else you could do."

Dallas brightened again, "I could call the neighbor lady and go over there."

"Okay. Here's her number."

Once more Dallas hung up looking dejected. "She's not going to be home." He looked thoughtful and then added, "I know! I can call Grandpa!" Dallas dialed his Grandpa and they talked for a few minutes. Hanging up the phone, he grinned from ear to ear and told Nola, "Grandpa will be here at nine o'clock!"

—— *C.C.M.*

On the worksheets on the following pages, practice inviting an alternative.

INVITING AN ALTERNATIVE AT WORK - EXAMPLE

1. **What is the expectation that the employee finds restrictive?**

   Voice mail greetings must be changed daily.

2. **What is the employee's objection?**

   If I am traveling, it is ridiculous to change it by long distance every day when the same message lasts the whole time I'm gone. Also, a general message about "away from my desk or on my phone" works most of the time.

3. **What is the employee's suggested alternative?**

   Before a trip, change it once to remain until I return; update it if I am not in the office for the day.

4. **What are required boundaries, such as impact on others, policies and procedures, and practicality? Are these valid reasons rather than your personal preferences?**

   Company policy requires that greetings must be current and imply availability.

5. **Is the suggested alternative within these boundaries?**

   ☒ Yes. Agree to try it.

   ☐ No. Review boundaries again.
   Consider additional alternatives and aim for consensus.

INUITING AN ALTERNATIUE AT HOME - EKAMPLE

1. **What is the expectation that the child finds restrictive?**

   Homework must be completed before dinner.

2. **What is the child's objection?**

   I want to play outside with my friends after school.

3. **What is the child's suggested alternative?**

   I could play outside for an hour after school and then do an hour of homework before dinner. After dinner I could do one more hour of homework.

4. **What are required boundaries, such as impact on others, policies and procedures, and practicality? Are these valid reasons rather than your personal preferences?**

   When I was a child, I had to do all my homework before dinner, but this is just a personal preference.

   In our family, we value being prepared for school or work, so homework must be completed before school the next day.

5. **Is the suggested alternative within these boundaries?**

   ☒ Yes. Agree to try it.

   ☐ No. Review boundaries again.
   Consider additional alternatives and aim for consensus.

INVITING AN ALTERNATIVE AT WORK - PRACTICE

1. **What is the expectation that the employee finds restrictive?**

    _____

    _____

    _____

2. **What is the employee's objection?**

    _____

    _____

    _____

3. **What is the employee's suggested alternative?**

    _____

    _____

    _____

4. **What are required boundaries, such as impact on others, policies and procedures, and practicality? Are these valid reasons rather than your personal preferences?**

    _____

    _____

    _____

5. **Is the suggested alternative within these boundaries?**

    ☐ Yes. Agree to try it.

    ☐ No. Review boundaries again.
       Consider additional alternatives and aim for consensus.

INVITING AN ALTERNATIVE AT HOME - PRACTICE

1. **What is the expectation that the child finds restrictive?**

    _____

    _____

    _____

2. **What is the child's objection?**

    _____

    _____

    _____

3. **What is the child's suggested alternative?**

    _____

    _____

    _____

4. **What are required boundaries, such as impact on others, policies and procedures, and practicality? Are these valid reasons rather than your personal preferences?**

    _____

    _____

    _____

5. **Is the suggested alternative within these boundaries?**

    ☐ Yes. Agree to try it.

    ☐ No. Review boundaries again.
    Consider additional alternatives and aim for consensus.

Conferencing Skill: Aim for Consensus

The conferencing strategy moves discussion toward consensus, encouraging agreement about a new, mutually satisfactory expectation. Sometimes, the employee or child suggests a workable alternative. However, when neither the original expectation nor the alternative will work, it takes a more complex discussion to achieve consensus. An employee's request to write sales manuals at home could work except for his isolation from the dynamics of the sales department. A fourteen-year-old's desire to walk to the mall with a friend after school instead of waiting for a parent to drive seems sensible except when the route parallels a major highway.

The mentor holds fast to the values of the organization or family. *Our training should reflect the realities of today's changing customer climate.* Or, *We value personal safety.* To achieve consensus, the mentor encourages brainstorming a variety of alternatives and assessing each option. The employee might regularly come into the office for sales staff meetings, and the two teenagers could ride the bus to the mall. Both the mentor and his employee or child must believe that some previously unconsidered possibility will improve the situation. They continue to ask each other *Can you live with that?* or *Will that work for you?* until both answer *Yes.*

> *I once agreed to consult with one side in a labor-management contract negotiation, primarily because I wanted to observe the consultant for the other side. Wallace was a well-respected, veteran negotiator, and I anticipated learning a great deal by watching him. When the meeting began, I was disappointed to see a young man from his staff in Wallace's place. The meeting dragged on into the wee hours, while each side made demands of the other.*
>
> *About two in the morning the young man slipped out, and a few minutes later Wallace arrived. He was fresh and clear-eyed, while we were exhausted. He opened discussion, and within an hour our negotiations*

were concluded. As we all left, I asked him what caused him to arrive at that exact moment: the late hour, his own schedule, or something else?

"I send someone to sit in for me with only one directive," Wallace explained. "He must listen carefully and call me when someone asks the first question of the other side. That's when I will come. You see, no real negotiation can take place while people are still focused on their own interests. Only when they ask what the other side wants and willingly listen to those needs can true negotiation occur."

—*L.C.D.*

During conferencing, you encourage a variety of ideas. Of course, you cannot accept suggestions that violate a law, a contractual arrangement, or a regulation of an outside agency. Your employee might complain *I think our company's rule about nepotism is absurd. My son would make a wonderful employee!* Your fifteen-year-old might protest *I don't understand why I can't see that movie just because of a stupid rating.* Yet, in both cases, at least you can respond in a way that validates feelings. To your employee, you can say *If I were you, I would be disappointed, too.* To your child you might reply *You'll be glad when you are seventeen.*

Without a valid reason to be against an idea, consider it. Explore all possibilities rather than rejecting an employee's or child's contributions. An employee who readily accepts the structure of the organization and commits to its basic values can participate in determining the standards for his performance.

Filing at the local abstract company had fallen behind, and Katherine, the office manager, announced that all nine women in the office would have to work overtime in the evenings to catch up. They immediately rebelled, "I have kids to pick up . . . . We've got ball practice . . . . My husband works the afternoon shift . . . ."

"Okay," Katherine acknowledged. "Let's talk about this. It's important to provide up-to-date information for our customers. I thought you

Chapter 4 - Conferencing

should stay late every evening when we get behind, but that doesn't sound too workable. What else would work for everyone?" Suggestions flew around the room with frequent rejections. Katherine summarized what she had heard. "It sounds like Saturdays work best for most people, except those with young children. And everyone is concerned about losing family time. Is that right?"

The group agreed and moved on to discuss what they might do to make Saturdays work. Their plan included the company's hiring a day care center director to entertain children during the morning in a second floor open area, providing pizza for everyone at noon, and giving everyone certificates for take-out barbecue dinners.

Everyone showed up on the selected Saturday. However, lunch had to be moved up to eleven-thirty because they had finished all the filing in record time.

—L.C.D.

Consensus differs from compromise. Compromise interferes with trusting relationships and establishes a pattern of winning and losing because those involved agree to take turns getting their way. Although expedient, this approach strongly convinces participants that every disagreement has a loser and requires renegotiation. *I cleaned up the dishes in the break room Friday.* Or, *I had to sleep on the couch the last time we had company!* As a mentor, you must aim past compromise to the more lasting agreements created by consensus. Even so, realize that striving for consensus will require candid communication, mutual trust, and a committed investment of time. Hidden agendas and attempts to manipulate preclude consensus.

Mansa was tired of hearing his children fight over who got to sit in the front seat of the car. Yet, when he enforced taking turns, they argued even more. He sat down with nine-year-old Rance and seven-year-old Olisa and explained that they must work things out between themselves and agree on a permanent plan for sharing the front seat.

168

The day after their conference, Rance and Olisa accompanied their father in the car to visit a friend. When it was time to leave, the two children stood outside the open car door whispering for several minutes.

"Okay," said Olisa as she climbed in the back seat. "We're ready to go!"

As Rance got in the front, Mansa smiled to his friend. "I don't know their plan, but they know if I hear them argue they both have to sit in back."

———————————————————— C.C.M.

Consensus redefines what it means to "win." Begin to think about meeting the values of your organization or family rather than getting your way. At work, promote a sense of teamwork and commitment among employees by mutually agreeing on common goals and objectives. At home, take advantage of this unique opportunity to teach your child how to collaborate with others. This approach to relationships will become part of his life experience and develop skills he can use on the school playground, the student council, and in his first job. Through conferencing, both of you will grow.

When Sawyer and his eleven-year-old daughter, Libby, disagreed, their voices got louder and louder until finally Sawyer yelled at Libby to go to her room. One day Libby asked Sawyer, "How come I'm the one who always has to go when you're the one who's mad?"

Sawyer answered, "Because I'm the Dad, and you can't talk disrespectfully to me." Even though he said it with confidence, Libby's question caused him to think. A few days later, Sawyer said to Libby, "I've been thinking about your question about why you always have to go to your room. I've always told you that I want you to be respectful, but it seems to me that I am not respectful when I yell."

Libby agreed, "Dad, you're always talking about respect. I've learned from you that respect is important. That's why I don't understand when you yell at me."

"You're right," Sawyer responded. "I can see how it makes you even more frustrated with me when I order you to your room. What could we do when we start yelling and being disrespectful to each other?"

As Sawyer and Libby discussed a variety of options, they began to realize that when they felt like they were beginning to be disrespectful to each other they must both walk away. Libby thought she would voluntarily go to her room and listen to music until she calmed down. Sawyer had never entertained the idea of walking away because it would have felt like Libby was "winning." But he began to think of going outside to cool down so that he could come back and model calm discussions with Libby. They agreed to put their plan into action: get distance when they started being disrespectful and then talk about the issue later when they were both calmer.

—— C.C.M.

Avoid conferencing in the heat of the moment or in the midst of disagreement. Anger hardens positions and blocks consensus. When upset about an expectation for behavior, it becomes difficult to envision alternatives. *I've worked overtime for the last three days, and I will not work overtime tonight.* Or, *Everyone else is going out after the dance Saturday night. There's no good reason why I can't, too.* Look for opportunities to conference respectfully in a calm moment. Sometimes, just looking for any point of agreement can break a deadlock.

A team of managers in a credit union had become deadlocked in their efforts to solve a problem with service charge billing cycles. Each person had hardened his position to the point that they were ready to disband in failure. I asked them to meet once more and this time to discuss their criteria for a perfect solution. They quickly agreed on five items: low cost, easy implementation, completion by the first of the month, compatibility with the current computer system, and simple explanation for customers.

Next, we listed every possible solution or course of action we could imagine. After the first few predictable "pet" solutions, others emerged. When we had about eight possibilities, I asked them to compare each one to their original criteria. Solution number five met every one of their criteria, though it was not one anyone had championed. I asked the team to reevaluate number five to be certain that it met their values. When it did, I asked, "So you're done? You have your solution?"

Pleased but stunned, they asked, "When did we agree? We haven't even fought yet."

—L.C.D.

When issues such as chores, allowance, or curfews relate to an individual child's behavior, conferencing is best handled privately. However, when such topics concern everyone in the family, regularly scheduled family meetings can present calm moments for communicating, sharing feelings, and revising expectations. Children especially look forward to a family meeting when it includes a positive experience, such as serving a favorite food, planning for a family outing, or playing a game. As children develop, they can more easily grasp the perspective of others. Family conferences can advance this ability.

Chandi and Philip felt as though they talked frequently with their sons, four-and-a-half-year-old Jalil and two-and-a-half-year-old Quinton, about their values of safety and respect. Yet, they also found themselves saying, "No hitting" and "Stop fighting" on a near-daily basis. Finally, they decided to sit down at the family dining table with the boys. Jalil and Quinton quickly identified the values of safety and respect as important, but they agreed that they had trouble living up to expectations. The family decided to write a set of "house rules" that they all could agree on. The boys dictated:

1. If there is a fire, get out quick.
2. If someone gets hurt, call 911.

3. Clean up the toys when you are done with them.

4. We don't hit each other.

5. If there's a gun in someone's house, don't touch it. Run and tell a grown-up.

6. Only adults touch the TV.

7. If a horse comes running at you, get out of the way.

8. Never stand on a swivel chair.

9. Always wipe up spills before someone slips and falls.

10. Toys go in the basket during meals.

11. If you get mad, go in your room and stay until you feel better.

Chandi told me, "What I am really proud of is number eleven. You may have to say it a million times and model it a million more, but number eleven coming out of Jalil's four-and-a-half-year-old mouth one day out of the blue is proof that it really does get through on some level. He thought it would be great to add this rule to our list. Wow!"

————————————————————————————— C.C.M.

In your role as a manager or parent, others look to you for guidance about how to negotiate differences. The conferencing strategy requires you to model maturity, openness, and genuine interest in the perspective of others. You validate the feelings of your employee or child about restrictive expectations, invite and accept suggestions for alternatives, and aim discussion toward new, mutually agreeable expectations.

The following examples and worksheets can further develop your consensus-building skills.

AIMING FOR CONSENSUS AT WORK - EXAMPLE

1. **What are the applicable values of the organization?**

   - *Hospitality to all guests*
   - *Fiscal responsibility*
   - *Efficiency*

2. **What is the current expectation?**

   The Guest Services Manager must call to welcome each guest within thirty minutes of check-in.

3. **What is the employee's objection?**

   This is time consuming, and I miss some guests who leave their rooms immediately after checking in.

4. **What are all the possible alternatives that the two of you can brainstorm?**

   - *Hire a greeter whose only job is to call guests*
   - *Include a welcome letter in each check-in packet*
   - *Guest Services Manager can call guests at random*

5. **Compare alternatives to organizational values.**

Greeter	*Not fiscally sound*
Welcome letter	*Not efficient for front desk staff, but housekeepers could leave a letter in rooms after preparing for new guests*
Random calls	*Does not ensure hospitality for all guests; not efficient use of time*

6. **What is the new expectation?**

   The Guest Services Manager will draft a welcome letter for house-keepers to leave in each room when preparing for new guests.

AIMING FOR CONSENSUS AT HOME - EXAMPLE

1. **What are the applicable values of the family?**

   - *Safety*
   - *Family communication*
   - *Increasing a child's responsibility*
   - *Downtime for parents*

2. **What is the current expectation?**

   Nicolette should be home within thirty minutes after the school basketball game is over.

3. **What is the child's objection?**

   I'm the only one who has a driver's license, and it takes time to drive my friends home after the basketball game.

4. **What are all the possible alternatives that the two of you can brainstorm?**

   - *Ask a parent to drive*
   - *Meet friends at the game*
   - *Invite all friends home to spend the night*
   - *Call parents when leaving the game and estimate arrival time*

5. **Compare alternatives to family values.**

Parent drives	*Does not teach responsibility; imposes on parents' downtime*
Meet friends	*Imposes on all parents' downtime*
Spend the night	*Imposes on parents' downtime*
Call parents	*Meets all values*

6. **What is the new expectation?**

   Nicolette will estimate how long it will take to drive her friends home and call on the cell phone when leaving the game.

AIMING FOR CONSENSUS AT WORK - PRACTICE

1. What are the applicable values of the organization?

   _____

   _____

2. What is the current expectation?

   _____

   _____

3. What is the employee's objection?

   _____

   _____

4. What are all the possible alternatives that the two of
   you can brainstorm?

   _____

   _____

   _____

5. Compare alternatives to organizational values.

   _____

   _____

   _____

6. What is the new expectation?

   _____

   _____

AIMING FOR CONSENSUS AT HOME - PRACTICE

1. **What are the applicable values of the family?**

    _____

    _____

2. **What is the current expectation?**

    _____

    _____

3. **What is the child's objection?**

    _____

    _____

4. **What are all the possible alternatives that the two of you can brainstorm?**

    _____

    _____

    _____

5. **Compare alternatives to family values.**

    _____

    _____

    _____

6. **What is the new expectation?**

    _____

    _____

Connecting the Mentoring Model: Conferencing and Coaching

Conferencing naturally produces new expectations. You conference with your employee or child when she feels that the established expectation has become too restrictive. Together, you determine a mutually acceptable expectation that meets the values of the organization or family.

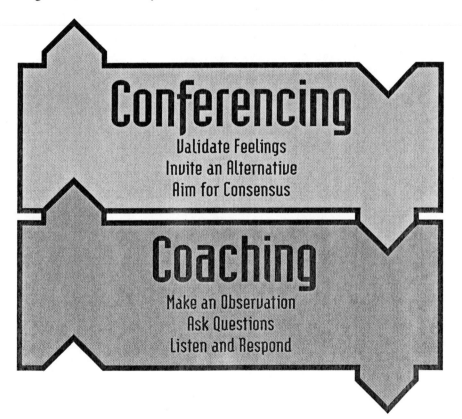

Conferencing
Validate Feelings
Invite an Alternative
Aim for Consensus

Coaching
Make an Observation
Ask Questions
Listen and Respond

After conferencing, always return to coaching to ensure the success of your employee or child as she learns how to meet the new expectation. You make observations, ask questions, listen and respond. However, this time the skills and techniques she develops will help her perform toward an expectation she has helped create.

177

Ask your employee *Now that we've agreed that you will wrap the parts before you sort them, is your wrapping machine still in the right place for you?* Say to your child *You're right. You are old enough to start baby-sitting now. How would you like to let our friends know that you're available?*

> *Two-year-old Tate expressed anger by hitting. His mother, Dawn, put him in his crib to get distance when she could not reason with him. As his language developed, Tate told Dawn that he didn't like being put in his crib. Dawn reminded him of the "no hitting" rule and asked Tate what else they could do when he got mad.*
>
> *At the end of their conference, they agreed that instead of going to his crib, Tate could use his words to describe to Dawn what he was mad about. If she understood the cause of his frustration, she could more easily help him.*
>
> *A few days later, Tate was mad about something and pulled back his arm to hit Dawn. She quickly returned to coaching. "Remember, 'no hitting,' Tate. What words can you use?"*
>
> *Pausing with arm in midair, Tate shouted, "I want to hit you!"*
>
> — C.C.M.

Sometimes, your conference points out that your employee or child simply needs more coaching. Your initial coaching may not have developed her skills to meet your expectation, and her resistance indicates she does not understand how to perform. When your employee repeatedly ignores your request for a complex report or argues about its importance, it may signal her reluctance to admit that she does not know how to prepare it. Hold yourself accountable for her inadequate skills, and quickly move back to coaching. When your nine-year-old son protests as you leave him at the local college for a summer basketball camp, conference to determine the cause for his emotion. Consider coaching him how to find the right building and introduce himself to the staff.

Bernice, the plant's director of Human Resources, put her lunch tray down on the cafeteria table. "Hi, Dodie," she said to the supervisor next to her, as she sat down.

"Hello, Bernice. Have you come to pester me about my job descriptions?"

"No, Dodie, I really came for lunch," Bernice smiled. "But now that you mention it, they are long overdue."

"I know you need them on all of my people and that they're important, but I'm lost every time I read instructions about 'essential functions' and 'physical requirements,'" Dodie confessed. "Jerry said you taught a class about all that ADA stuff when it came out, but I wasn't a supervisor back then."

"So, you never had any training about how to write job descriptions?" Bernice asked.

Dodie shook her head.

"Would it help if I spent some time with you this afternoon, showing you the materials from that class? We've got a video that you could take home and watch, too," Bernice suggested.

"That would be great, Bernice. Thanks," Dodie agreed. "Then, I'll get those job descriptions written for you as quickly as I can!'

—L.C.D.

Some expectations must remain inflexible regardless of how strongly the employee or child disagrees. Existing expectations may have certain requirements embedded in a law, regulation, or other circumstance. A bakery employee cannot expect to make bread with her hair uncovered. You reaffirm the organization's expectation and move from conferencing about her disagreement back to coaching about various techniques to cover her hair. A teenager with only a learner's permit may not drive alone, no matter how much she pleads. You acknowledge her feelings, remind her of the legal expectation, and continue to coach her driving skills.

Ramona had recently been transferred to Nolan's section of the drafting firm in hopes that he could help her meet the firm's expectations more appropriately. An older, assertive person, Ramona had intimidated her previous supervisors and alienated her coworkers with her disregard for the rules and procedures of the firm.

"Hey, Nolan, what's this about having to have the Phoenix project in on time? You know I work at my own pace, and I'll get it done eventually," Ramona began. Coming into his office, she sat in a chair by the door. "What's the big deal about somebody else's deadlines anyway?"

"Ramona, I'm not sure we've been quite fair with you in the past about deadlines," Nolan said. "Perhaps we've never made it clear how important they are or how others are depending on you to complete your part of each project. But, from now on, you must meet each of your deadlines. If it will help, I'll work with you on planning more accurately. Would you be interested in going to a project planning seminar?"

"Am I in trouble for something I did in the past?" Ramona asked, starting to become concerned.

"No," Nolan assured her. "We're not talking about the past. You and I have a chance to work together now, and I want you to understand what I expect. Now, about a project planning seminar . . . ."

—*L.C.D.*

You may also recognize the need to return to coaching when your employee or child cannot or will not participate fully in a conference. A very young child may not have the language skills to conference. Older children or some adults may feel embarrassed to acknowledge emotions or admit their lack of skill. Even when you validate feelings, anger and resentment may inhibit a productive conference. Allow your employee or child time to cool down before you recommence coaching.

Eight-year-old Ryder was mad at his three-year-old sister, Holly, and retaliated by cutting out a huge piece of her hair. Recognizing that Ryder was full of anger, his father, Steven, began a conference. "Ryder, you must have been extremely angry to have hurt Holly in this way."

As they conferenced, Ryder talked about his anger. Steven then moved the conversation toward a plan for making reparation to Holly. He believed that making amends taught a child the value of regret more than simply saying "I'm sorry." Steven expected his children to work out a heartfelt plan, such as giving a hug, writing a letter, or taking flowers.

"So, Ryder, what do you want to do to make this up to Holly?" Steven asked.

"Nothing," Ryder replied.

"Why don't you think about it tonight, then, and we'll talk again in the morning," Steven concluded.

The next morning, Steven asked Ryder, "What idea have you come up with?"

"I don't want to think of anything!" Ryder replied.

"Well, then, Ryder," Steven coached, "let's talk about how you can buy her a flower."

—C.C.M.

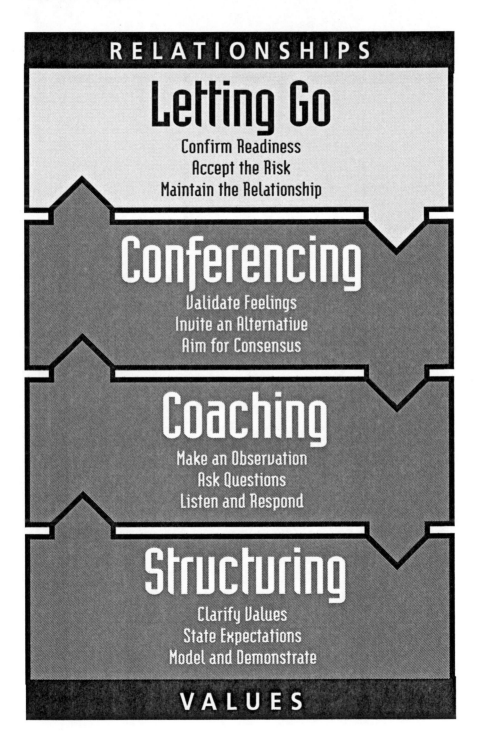

RELATIONSHIPS

Letting Go
Confirm Readiness
Accept the Risk
Maintain the Relationship

Conferencing
Validate Feelings
Invite an Alternative
Aim for Consensus

Coaching
Make an Observation
Ask Questions
Listen and Respond

Structuring
Clarify Values
State Expectations
Model and Demonstrate

VALUES

CHAPTER FIVE

Letting Go

By **Letting Go,** the mentor transfers complete control for appropriate behavior. Your focus shifts from expanding expectations to recognizing responsibility and self-direction. You move beyond control when your employee or child chooses the values, expectations, and skills that define the **why, what,** and **how** of her own behavior. As a mentor, you continue to believe in the values of your organization or family and choose to maintain a supportive relationship with your employee or child.

YOUR LETTING GO SCORE

Items ten through twelve on the self-tests in Chapter One indicate your approach to **letting go.** Transfer your answers from those items to the box on the next page. Add your scores vertically. Compare your letting go scores to the descriptions of the four letting go styles that follow.

Items Related to Letting Go

SELF-TEST FOR WORK

10.	a _____	b _____	d _____	c _____
11.	c _____	b _____	a _____	d _____
12.	b _____	a _____	c _____	d _____
TOTALS	_____	_____	_____	_____
	BOSS	MANIPULATOR	MARTYR	MENTOR

SELF-TEST FOR HOME

10.	a _____	b _____	d _____	c _____
11.	c _____	b _____	a _____	d _____
12.	b _____	a _____	c _____	d _____
TOTALS	_____	_____	_____	_____
	BOSS	MANIPULATOR	MARTYR	MENTOR

HOW EACH STYLE LETS GO

The **boss** cannot let go of making choices for her employee or child. She does not consider his readiness to make responsible or trustworthy decisions and views his growing independence as resistance or insubordination. Her effort to maintain control either perpetuates his dependence or further alienates him to the point of severance or impasse. The boss manager fuels resentment among all employees, eventually driving the competent ones away. *Travis was* *always going off on his own without asking me!* The boss parent continues to assume that she must control the child, even nagging adult children about their physical appearance, employment status, or financial situation. *You just need to lose all that weight.*

The **manipulator** lets go by giving up. He no longer can control the choices made by his employee or child because he has few incentives left to give. The manipulator has taught her to value rewards and avoid punishment. She has learned to make behavioral choices based on goodies and to value things, not relationships. Therefore, relationships stop when the goodies stop. Conceding to his demanding employees causes the manipulator manager finally to reach the end of his budget and his resourcefulness. *Marjo is at the top of her pay scale, and we've bought her a new computer. I don't know what else we can do to make her stay.* At home, the child grows to expect money, cars, trips, and jewelry. The parent fears that the child faces failure without "motivation." *I'm afraid that Chase won't be successful if I'm not there to motivate him.*

The **martyr** continuously lets go. Her employees and children choose their own behavior, regardless of the values of the organization or family. She overlooks or excuses inappropriate behavior, seeking appreciation and recognition in her relationships. The martyr manager, bewildered by an employee's lack of gratitude, complains *After all I've done for Greta . . . .* The martyr parent has little direct, positive impact on the behavior of her independent children. As they get older, she may ultimately become irrelevant. *The children never come to see me anymore.*

The **mentor** lets go by moving beyond a focus on controlling behavior. He encourages responsibility and self-direction after confirming the readiness of employees and children to choose their own values. He trusts their initiative and skills, nurtured through his systematic preparation. The mentor values cultivating a mentoring relationship with his employees and children and views letting go as a positive growth experience for everyone. The mentor manager delights in the success of his employees. *Rashid, coming up with a* *new way to package that shipment of antique glassware showed that you heard the customer's concern.* The mentor parent recognizes the ethics and responsibility involved when her eighteen-year-old does not ask for money. *I respect you for choosing to work an extra job to earn the money for the deductible after your car accident.*

LETTING GO AS A STRATEGY

When an employee or child makes appropriate choices that indicate his understanding of the values of the organization or family, the mentor can let go. When she coached, she let go of **how** he performed; when she conferenced, she let go of **what** the organization or family expected. Now she must let go of **why** he behaves as he does. After letting go, the mentor no longer makes choices on behalf of her employee or child. She has moved beyond control.

As her employee or child begins to make choices based on values, the mentor observes his behavior and compares it to values of the organization or family. When his behavior consistently matches a specific value over time, she can conclude that he has internalized that value and confirm his readiness to make his own value-based choice for that particular issue. The retirement home cook who routinely plans food purchases within the budget demonstrates his commitment to fiscal accountability. When a high school student chooses to spend his weekend completing a term paper instead of going on a ski trip with his friends, the parent knows that her son has internalized the value of time management.

Grace and her seventeen-year-old daughter, Noelle, went shopping for a dress for the upcoming prom. They found a tasteful dress that suited Noelle's age and even found shoes and gloves to match. By the end of the day, they had purchased everything except earrings.

Before Grace left for work the next day, she gave Noelle money to shop for earrings suitable for the dress. Eager to see Noelle's purchase, Grace was surprised when Noelle came home that evening without earrings. Noelle explained, "Mom, every time I looked at a pair, I could just hear your voice in my head saying, 'Don't let the earrings cheapen the dress.'"

———————————————————— C.C.M.

When an employee arrives at the workplace already committed to an organizational value, his manager can quickly let go. If a new realtor already takes part in a civic club's pancake breakfast and belongs to the local Chamber of Commerce, his choice to become involved in the community indicates his personal belief in the organization's values of civic responsibility and volunteerism. However, if a new realtor shows no interest in civic involvement, his manager needs to teach him its importance. By coaching him how to balance work and outside activities and by conferencing when he has difficulty, a manager can develop the realtor's civic responsibility.

Parents often think that letting go happens when a child grows up and leaves home. However, letting go occurs bit by bit for years. The mentor evaluates how the child behaves the first time he spends the entire night away from home, unsuccessfully tries out for the junior high school tennis team, and drives his friends in the car on a Friday night. The child gradually internalizes a variety of values and increasingly takes control of his choices. As the mentor observes value-based behaviors, the child earns more freedom, his limits expand, and the mentor continues to let go one issue at a time.

In most instances, employees and children internalize the values modeled by mentor managers and mentor parents. An employee or child may become responsible and self-directed with little effort on the mentor's part. *Once Valerie understood our value of cleanliness, she always wiped the break room counter after her lunch.* Or, *After Grant learned how to trim his fingernails, he kept them neatly trimmed from then on.* Suddenly, the mentor realizes that she has let go of that specific issue.

Nine-year-old Delaney and six-year-old Morton routinely went to bed at seven-thirty each evening. Their parents, George and Jeanne, had often discussed with them the value of a good night's sleep and believed that this contributed to the lack of problems at bedtime. After the children began to realize that their friends stayed up later, George and Jeanne told them that bedtime was now their responsibility. That night at seven-thirty, George looked at Jeanne and said, "I think I'm going to hit the sack. I'm tired and want to get a good night's sleep."

Jeanne yawned and replied, "I think I'll go to bed, too. I have a big day at work tomorrow and want to be rested so that I can do my best."

George and Jeanne got up to go to their bedroom and kissed the children goodnight. Delaney and Morton looked at each other and then got up and went to their bedrooms as well. Bedtime never became a problem in George and Jeanne's household.

———————————————————————— C.C.M.

Letting go obligates the mentor to give the employee or child complete responsibility for his choices and their results. If a manager or parent criticizes, complains, or reclaims ownership, she diminishes trust and damages the relationship. When an employee chooses to open his staff meeting for honest discussion, his manager refrains from commenting *I wouldn't do that. Asking people for their opinions just means trouble.* The mentor willingly separates herself, accepting the potential of an uncertain outcome. When a fifteen-year-old loans his skateboard to a friend who breaks it, his parent says *That's too bad* instead of *I told you that boy doesn't take care of things.*

Melissa's duties as director of development for a large charity included arranging monthly board meetings. As she reviewed the table placement, meal selection, and agenda for the day's meeting, her phone rang.

"Melissa," began Howard, the charity's president. "I'm calling about the board meeting. What color napkins do you plan to use?"

"What color napkins?" she asked. "I don't know—whatever the caterer brings, I guess."

"Well, tell him to bring all the colors he has, and I'll come early to pick one," Howard insisted. "Everything must be just right for our board meetings, you know."

—L.C.D.

When she lets go, the mentor risks that her employee or child may adopt values that conflict with those of the organization or family. Despite the urge to interpret a different choice as a challenge to authority, she respects her employee or child enough to consider the potential of his new choices. His experience, skill, and judgment convinced her of his readiness; now she must trust that his ideas may represent a valid perspective. When a grocery store manager desires to reduce personnel costs by closing at midnight, his commitment to fiscal stability may outweigh the owner's belief in all-night service. When a son dries his pup tent in the front yard, his reliability for maintaining his camping equipment may surpass his mother's need for orderliness.

Chantal was in junior high and beginning to do her own laundry. Her mother, Marini, valued neat appearance and showed her how to carefully sort clothes by color and select proper washing and drying temperatures. Then, Marini transferred the responsibility to Chantal and did not think about it again.

One Saturday morning before Chantal left for play practice, Marini noticed that the washer was crammed to overflowing with both white clothes and jeans. She refrained from saying anything, but later she observed that the dry white clothes, now slightly blue, appeared to have shrunk. All were extremely wrinkled. Marini could hold her tongue no longer, "Chantal, you dried your clothes too long."

Chantal cheerfully replied, "Oh, that's okay, Mom. I like them extra crispy!"

— C.C.M.

Sometimes, the employee or child selects a conflicting value that the organization or family cannot ignore. When his choice interferes with the work of the organization or disrupts the life of the family, the mentor evaluates its impact and addresses the issue in a conference. The mentor opens the conference by validating feelings within the current situation. *I know you take pride in entering accurate data . . . . I'm worried about your getting behind.* Or, *You must have been in a big hurry to play ball with your friends after school . . . . Your little brother walked home alone.* The mentor responds to suggested alternatives, expanding expectations to meet both values when possible. *That's a good plan, to check every entry only once before you move on.* Or, *Okay, after you walk him across all the streets, you can go play ball once he is on our block.*

> *Ned and Lucinda complained that last year thirteen-year-old A.J. mowed the lawn all summer without being told, but this summer despite their nagging he chose to spend his time watching TV. I suggested that they conference with A.J. about the conflicting values of helping around the house and relaxing. I encouraged them to search for an expectation for A.J.'s summer that met both values.*
>
> *The next week Ned and Lucinda reported that in their conference A.J. explained that he didn't mind helping around the house, but he was tired of mowing the lawn. He agreed instead to keep the dog waste picked up out of the yard. Although both parents suspected that they would end up nagging him about this new expectation, A.J. picked up the waste all week without being told and still had time for his favorite TV shows.*
>
> *I asked Ned and Lucinda to continue to think of A.J. as the "dog waste expert" and show interest in his work. At the next session, Ned reported that he had asked A.J. why he had two shovels and was impressed when A.J. explained that the flat one worked better on the concrete, while the rounded shovel worked better on the grass.*
>
> —C.C.M.

Even in the face of conflicting values, the mentor can choose to maintain a relationship with her employee or child. Recognizing his responsibility and self-direction does not end her mentoring relationship. Sharing his vulnerability in failure and his pride in success can build a deep relationship and forge a lifelong bond.

Letting Go at Work

The culture of an organization requires certain behaviors, and managers often assume that employees know why. As a result, they may fail to talk to their employees about organizational values. *These are adults; I shouldn't have to tell them everything.* Or, *They've worked here long enough to know better.*

> *Leonard, the bank president, was typing a letter when I arrived for our five-thirty appointment. "I've got to correct this before I can sign it," he explained with exasperation. "Before she left for the day, my secretary gave it to me for my signature. But it had some typos in it. She should know we can't send out letters with typos. I'm getting real tired of staying late to retype letters before I can send them out."*
>
> —L.C.D.

Letting go obligates a manager to structure, coach, and conference as a prerequisite. If a manager overlooks any of these strategies, he contributes to the frustration or failure of his employees rather than to their success. In the end, the manager will spend more energy dealing with inaccuracy and ineptness than he would have exerted in mentoring.

> *Ritter, the owner of the local sporting goods store, was furious! "I leave for a few minutes to get coffee, and when I get back, look . . . ." He pointed to a burned out fluorescent light bulb over a prominent display of sweatshirts. He gathered a ladder and a new bulb from the storeroom, climbed up, and replaced the old bulb.*

While he worked, he complained to no one in particular, "I don't know why you people can't see that a light bulb is out and change it! I shouldn't have to do everything around here myself!" His staff paid little attention to him, dismissing his tantrum as "Just Ritter!"

—*L.C.D.*

Adults arrive in the workplace with personal values that will influence their professional behavior. Sometimes, a manager only has to recognize or refine values that coincide with those of the organization; sometimes, he has to challenge inappropriate existing values. An employee who picks up her tools, stores equipment, and routinely mops up spills, reflects her commitment to the organization's value of safety. On the other hand, a mechanic may understand the need for tact and courtesy when explaining repairs to customers but may fail to live up to those standards.

Both the manager and the employee must accept the results of the employee's choices. Failing to identify with the organization's values, such as timeliness, personal responsibility, trustworthiness, quality, or quantity of work may cause an employee not to get a raise or promotion. It may even cause her to lose her job. In essence, she may fire herself by ignoring or deliberately rejecting non-negotiable values. Yet, when an employee makes a different value choice, she still deserves respect and courtesy. Even if the professional relationship ends, a mentor may choose to continue a personal relationship with his former employee. In today's work environment, personal relationships easily rekindle new professional ones.

Letting Go At Home

A parent can easily become trapped by her own dreams. *I always wanted to play the piano, so I'm going to enroll Evan in piano lessons.* Or, *I want Julie to be a cheerleader in high school, so I'm signing her up for gymnastics now.* The parent must recognize that these dreams relate to her own needs, and that she can take piano lessons or join an adult gymnastics program instead of projecting her dreams onto her child. When the parent models her own enjoyment of piano or gymnastics, her child will more likely value it as well. The child must grow into his own person by discovering his own passions.

> *Cal grew up loving baseball and dreamed of the day when he would have a son who would love it as well. When David turned five and could join a T-ball team, Cal saw his dream coming true.*
>
> *David, however, confided in his mother that he liked playing ball but would rather have more time in the summer to ride his bike and play with his friends. Knowing this would be difficult for Cal to accept, David's mom advised him to tell his dad.*
>
> *Fortunately, Cal recognized that his dream was personal and did not condemn David's reluctance to join the T-ball team. David spent the summer riding his bike, playing with his friends, and hitting baseballs in the backyard with his family.*
>
> *When one of his friends asked David why he was not playing T-ball, he confidently replied, "Because I wanted to have more time to ride my bike and play with my friends this summer."*
>
> — *C.C.M.*

The mentor parent's approach to each day must reflect enjoyment of her child's companionship. Believing that his parent likes to spend time with him contributes to a child's self-worth. *I've missed you because I've been so busy at work this week. May I pick you up at school tomorrow and take you for lunch?*

> *Elaine came to counseling concerned about "motivating" her ten-year-old son, Charlie. As we talked, I discovered that Elaine focused on Charlie's performance in school and in sports. She rarely took time to talk with him about his dreams or his feelings about school and sports; Charlie complained that she didn't listen to him or try to understand him. I suggested that she occasionally invite Charlie for hot cocoa and just talk to him in an effort to get to know him better.*

Within a few days, Elaine took Charlie to the orthodontist before school. On the drive back to school, Elaine realized her opportunity to stop for hot cocoa and talk. Without sharing her idea with Charlie, she pulled the car in to the local coffee shop. Further convinced that his mother did not understand him, Charlie cried, "What are you doing? I'm going to be late for school!"

— *C.C.M.*

A parent must unconditionally accept her child before she will ever let go successfully. The child must believe that she loves him for himself, rather than for any potential to accomplish. He must know that she respects his unique thoughts and feelings and trusts his ability to choose values. A mentor encourages her child to live with confidence, enthusiasm, and initiative.

LETTING GO SKILLS

The letting go strategy transfers complete control for appropriate behavior to the employee or child. As a mentor, you recognize responsibility and self-direction when you practice the following three skills.

Letting Go
Confirm Readiness
Accept the Risk
Maintain the Relationship

Letting Go Skill: Confirm Readiness

Before you can confirm the readiness of your employee or child to make value-based choices, assess your own willingness to move beyond control. Your hesitancy to let go will undermine his chances for success and diminish his self-confidence. An editor questions a journalist's creativity when she rewrites his lead paragraph to fit her style. A father damages his ten-year-old daughter's belief in herself when he encourages her to call for a pizza and then criticizes her telephone manners.

Betty, the office manager of a title insurance company, expressed her frustration with employees who constantly interrupted her with questions about office procedures. "They keep asking for a written manual to illustrate and explain routine procedures, but I don't have the time to do it! Writing a manual would add to my workload!"

We discussed the importance of a manual to her employees and found that they were ready to participate in its creation, even if she was not. Two weeks later, Betty proudly reported that she had asked pairs of employees to address specific confusing office procedures and to research appropriate solutions. Each written response became a page in the office team's new procedures manual.

—L.C.D.

Letting go represents growth for the mentor, as well as for the employee or child. As you relinquish more and more responsibility for his behavior, you can explore your own new directions. However, this opportunity for personal development may feel unsettling if you have defined yourself primarily by your relationship to your employee or child. At work, you may question your own job security as your employee matures, perceiving his success as a threat to your position. After coaching every ball team for your children, you may initially feel unneeded in an "empty nest" and wonder how to fill your time.

When you make the determination to let go of a particular issue, you review your use of each of the mentoring strategies, trusting that you have shaped the values of your employees or children. At first, you modeled and demonstrated the value-based behaviors expected by your organization or family. As you structured, you controlled the choices of inexperienced employees or children. Different from the boss who imposes values without explanation, you taught essential beliefs of the organization or family as part of a systematic plan. *Gail, our consulting firm promotes teamwork, so each of us will present part of our proposal.* Or, *Justin, come with me to empty the wastebaskets and take the garbage cans to the curb. The garbage collection service comes early in the morning, and we want to be ready.*

Once employees and children began to choose their own techniques, you coached to develop their skills. *Would it give that part more emphasis if you stand up during your presentation?* Or, *Where will you keep the garbage bags so that it is most convenient for you?* When traditional expectations became too restrictive, you conferenced in order to expand the limits of their choices. *It sounds to me as though you'd like to present the conclusion by yourself next time.* Or, *As long as the garbage is at the curb on time, your idea of doing it before the school bus comes might work.* Throughout, your goal as a mentor was to help people internalize the values of the organization or family. Now recognizing their responsibility and self-direction, you let go. *Gail, here's your chance to put together a team and develop a proposal for our new client.* Or, *Justin, you've gotten the garbage out every week for the past six months. You must be proud of that!*

> *Candace supervised sixteen hospital emergency room nurses who last year had often changed their minds about summer vacation dates. As a result, Candace had revised the schedule continually throughout the summer.*
>
> *In early May, Candace called everyone to the conference room and explained, "Remember when we agreed last fall that we would each*

schedule our own days off and trade among ourselves when necessary. That new system has worked very well. In the past, I've scheduled summer vacations for the department, but this year we need to cooperate as a team to schedule them. Let's use our daily shift agreement as a guide: we select by seniority, with no more than two nurses off at a time."

"On the wall is a summer calendar and a list of nurses by seniority," she continued. *"James, you have the most seniority, so here's the marker. When you've written your choice on the calendar, pass the marker to the next person. After everyone has selected a vacation time, anyone may ask to trade days. We have three days before the schedule is due."*

With that, Candace left the room. After a slow start, the group completed the entire summer schedule by the end of the day.

—L.C.D.

Quite often your employee or child has the skill, ability, or potential to make his own choices before you recognize his readiness. Until time pressure or a new priority diverts your attention, you may fail to consider letting go. At work, you can create more time for your own new assignment when you realize that Tanya can monitor her personal work quality. When a new baby arrives in your home, you reassess the potential readiness of your school-age child to fold the family laundry and make a salad for dinner.

When her mother moved to a nearby nursing home, Nancy began to feel overwhelmed. Driving her daughter to ball games already filled her early evenings after work. Now Mom needed help with medications and adjustment to her new situation. Nancy called sixteen-year-old Ellis and thirteen-year-old Sharon together for a family meeting.

"Taking care of Grandma is going to take a lot more of my time than I thought," Nancy explained. "Some days I'm not going to be able to drive Sharon to her ball games. Ellis, from now on can you leave early enough to take her before you go to yours?"

"Sure, Mom," Ellis replied. "It's about time you let me drive some more!"

————————————————————————————— *C.C.M.*

Once you recognize your own readiness to let go, observe the behavior of your employee or child. Compare what you see to important values of your organization or family. Consider the following factors to help you confirm his readiness to make value-based choices.

Confirming Readiness

1. **Competence**

2. **Maturity**

3. **Trust**

4. **Developmental Level**

---

1. Competence

Evaluate the skill and experience of your employee or child. Do his actions reflect a strong commitment to a value? Especially notice how he makes decisions or solves problems under pressure. Your observation that Barry always listens respectfully to customer complaints shows his devotion to good service. Does your employee or child use shortcuts to increase efficiency or merely to avoid effort? When Colette wipes her hands on a towel instead of washing them, she shows a weak commitment to cleanliness.

Has your employee or child experienced a situation often enough to reveal his beliefs? The dental hygienist who frequently produces unreadable patient x-rays demonstrates an inconsistent approach to accuracy. When fourteen-year-old Jeralyn frequently stops after school to visit with elderly neighbors, she indicates an internalized value of respect.

Young David wanted to learn his parents' construction trade skills, but his eagerness outweighed his abilities. His mother, Mimi, selected the preparation of sheetrock walls as his first assignment. After demonstrating the process, she coached him in order to develop his techniques, while stressing the importance of quality workmanship. While his skills developed, his assigned walls were in the closets of each new house.

David worked to perfect his techniques and conferenced with his mother about different, newer tools. Over the next three years, David proved to Mimi that he could prepare the smoothest closet walls anywhere! From then on, Mimi entrusted David with all sheetrock preparation in each new house.

—L.C.D.

2. Maturity

Personal maturity, more than age, influences readiness to make value-based choices. A younger employee may make more mature decisions than a seasoned worker; some children can solve problems more effectively than their parents.

When Manda was in the sixth grade, she announced that she was going to become a vegetarian. "I don't like the taste of meat, and I hate the thought of killing animals. Mrs. Landry is a vegetarian, and she told me about other food you can eat for protein."

Manda's mother, Zita, valued good nutrition and was concerned about Manda's health, as well as how this would affect meal preparation. Manda began learning about complementary proteins and planning how to modify family meals. Zita realized that even though Manda was only twelve, she had made a thoughtful decision consistent with good nutrition.

— C.C.M.

As you evaluate maturity, also assess how your employee or child solves problems, responds to change, reacts to disappointment, and handles stress. At work, Rick's quick temper when things do not go his way in team meetings alerts you to continue conferencing with him about teamwork. However, Midori's habit of highlighting all policy revisions in her reference notebook indicates her mature adaptability to change.

At home, when Ethan refuses to return to school after classmates tease him, you recognize his immaturity in situations requiring courage. You appreciate fifteen-year-old Stephen's respect for public property when he chooses to return home instead of going to spray paint the water tower with his friends.

3. Trust

Trust in your employee or child builds over time. His earned reliability and credibility will prove his readiness to make his own choices. When his words and actions match consistently, you can let go. At work, when Shirley responds promptly to e-mails and returns phone calls by the end of each day, she reliably demonstrates her commitment to communication. At home, your latchkey child assures you that he turns in every assignment; yet, a teacher's note about missing homework causes you to question his credibility.

The issue of trust often has its roots in early childhood. When you see four-year-old Marshall standing in the pantry with chocolate around his mouth, you may want to ask *Have you been eating candy?* However, your question puts him in a position where he can easily avoid the truth by mumbling *No.* Instead, observing *I see you have been snacking before dinner* helps Marshall develop his trustworthiness. As a mentor, when you trust employees and children, you encourage them to respond in kind. Mistrusting people encourages their deception.

After fifteen years of experience, Terrill became the manager of Human Resources at a trucking firm. On his second day of work, he wanted to put a form in a personnel file. Expecting those files to be confidential, he began looking for a key. Finding none, Terrill searched for the files themselves. Finally, he asked the office manager about the files.

"Oh! Mary, the comptroller, has those in her office. She's kept the key in her purse for years. We have to ask her for it every time we want access to the personnel files."

—*L.C.D.*

4. Developmental Level

Mentor parents often consider a child's developmental level, as well as his age. Notably, readiness to make value-based choices depends on a child's capacity to think in terms of values. At first, your child makes choices simply based on what he wants. *I want to play with my new red fire truck all by myself.* He has to accept parental expectations about sharing and know what it feels like to share before he can internalize your parental value of cooperation. When you mentor, you teach your child to make choices for reasons other than his personal wants. As he develops, picking up trash with the Boy Scouts on Saturday mornings becomes less about wanting to sleep late and more about community service.

A child can make choices before he internalizes relevant values. Offer him choices that promote your values. *Do you want to shower at night or in the morning?* gives your child a choice between two expectations that each fulfill your family's value of personal hygiene. As he behaves according to your expectations, he will come to believe in your values as well.

Dinnertime had become a disaster. Kirsten and Roy described how four-year-old Lane's behavior disrupted the meal for everyone. When they placed his plate in front of him, Lane would scream that he hated the food, refuse to eat, and sometimes throw food across the room.

Kirsten and Roy were surprised at my suggestion that they serve family-style so that Lane could serve his own plate. They had not considered that he wanted to be more independent and was ready to serve himself. The next night Kirsten and Roy discussed the new system with Lane. A week later they were amazed that Lane was serving his own plate and eating a good dinner without complaining.

Two weeks later Kirsten and Roy reported that they had brought home Chinese take-out for dinner, and Lane had wanted to try a sample from every carton!

— *C.C.M.*

Confirming readiness can be practiced with the examples and worksheets on the following pages.

CONFIRMING READINESS AT WORK - EXAMPLE

Describe the situation: *Amory is a computer technician who has only worked here six months but who has three years' previous experience.*

Applicable value: *quantity of work*

1. Is your employee **competent** and committed to this applicable value of the organization? Does your employee:

    ☒ Make good decisions under pressure?

    ☒ Use shortcuts to increase efficiency? *Works two similar jobs at once*

    ☒ Exhibit positive patterns of behavior? *Stays late to finish jobs*

2. Is your employee **mature**? Does your employee:

    ☒ Solve problems effectively?

    ☐? Respond well to change? *No changes since he's been here*

    ☒ React favorably to disappointment?

    ☒ Handle stress appropriately? *Adapts to high work volume*

3. Has your employee earned **trust**? Does your employee:

    ☒ Match words and actions consistently? *Lives up to promises*

    ☒ Demonstrate commitment reliably?

    ☒ Behave in a credible manner?

4. Can you confirm your employee's **readiness** to become responsible and self-directed, consistent with the values of the organization?

    ☒ Yes. Let go and allow your employee to make personal choices.

    ☐ No. Conference about your concerns.

CONFIRMING READINESS AT HOME - EXAMPLE

Describe the situation: *Meghan promises her preschool age brother that she will play a game with him each day when she comes home from middle school.*

Applicable value: *kindness*

1. Is your child **competent** and committed to this applicable value of the family? Does your child:

   ☒ Make good decisions under pressure? *Explains when she has a test*

   ☒ Use shortcuts to increase efficiency? *Plays a fast game on a busy day*

   ☐ Exhibit positive patterns of behavior? *Forgets to tell him if she stays late at school*

2. Is your child **mature**? Does your child:

   ☒ Solve problems effectively? *Helps him find a game in allotted time*

   ☐ Respond well to change? *Doesn't let him know if change in plans*

   ☐ React favorably to disappointment? *Pouts if friend calls during game*

   ☐ Handle stress appropriately? *Not kind when brother begs for one more game*

3. Has your child earned **trust**? Does your child:

   ☐ Match words and actions consistently? *Says she'll be home but isn't*

   ☐ Demonstrate commitment reliably? *Not all days*

   ☐ Behave in a credible manner? *Doesn't show up some days*

4. Is your child **developmentally able** to make value-based choices?

   ☐ No. Offer choices among value-based expectations.

   ☒ Yes. Move to number 5 to confirm readiness.

5. Can you confirm your child's **readiness** to become responsible and self-directed, consistent with the values of the family?

   ☐ Yes. Let go and allow your child to make personal choices.

   ☒ No. Conference about your concerns.

CONFIRMING READINESS AT WORK - PRACTICE

Describe the situation: _____

_____

_____

Applicable value: _____

1. Is your employee **competent** and committed to this applicable value of the organization? Does your employee:

    ☐ Make good decisions under pressure?

    ☐ Use shortcuts to increase efficiency?

    ☐ Exhibit positive patterns of behavior?

2. Is your employee **mature**? Does your employee:

    ☐ Solve problems effectively?

    ☐ Respond well to change?

    ☐ React favorably to disappointment?

    ☐ Handle stress appropriately?

3. Has your employee earned **trust**? Does your employee:

    ☐ Match words and actions consistently?

    ☐ Demonstrate commitment reliably?

    ☐ Behave in a credible manner?

4. Can you confirm your employee's **readiness** to become responsible and self-directed, consistent with the values of the organization?

    ☐ Yes. Let go and allow your employee to make personal choices.

    ☐ No. Conference about your concerns.

CONFIRMING READINESS AT HOME - PRACTICE

Describe the situation: _____

_____

_____

Applicable value: _____

1. Is your child **competent** and committed to this applicable value of the family? Does your child:

    ☐ Make good decisions under pressure?

    ☐ Use shortcuts to increase efficiency?

    ☐ Exhibit positive patterns of behavior?

2. Is your child **mature**? Does your child:

    ☐ Solve problems effectively?

    ☐ Respond well to change?

    ☐ React favorably to disappointment?

    ☐ Handle stress appropriately?

3. Has your child earned **trust**? Does your child:

    ☐ Match words and actions consistently?

    ☐ Demonstrate commitment reliably?

    ☐ Behave in a credible manner?

4. Is your child **developmentally able** to make value-based choices?

    ☐ No.   Offer choices among value-based expectations.

    ☐ Yes. Move to number 5 to confirm readiness.

5. Can you confirm your child's **readiness** to become responsible and self-directed, consistent with the values of the family?

    ☐ Yes. Let go and allow your child to make personal choices.

    ☐ No.   Conference about your concerns.

Letting Go Skill: Accept the Risk

Once you have confirmed the readiness of your employee or child, you let go. Her choices are now beyond your control. Because you have consistently emphasized the values of your organization or family, for the most part she will have internalized them. You have minimized the risk that your employee or child might believe in a different value, and you worry little about outcomes because you share the same commitment. She will still experience life's inevitable ups and downs, make mistakes, or use poor judgment. But remember, your employee or child can become responsible and self-directed only when you let go and allow her to learn from her own experience.

> *The bank allowed Lynn, a vice president, to administer its charitable and community donations, but required that she secure the president's approval for each check. One morning Arlen, the president, came into her office to visit.*
>
> *"You do so well with our contributions that I think you should handle the whole process from now on," Arlen told her. "You've kept within the budget, and you've contributed throughout the community."*
>
> *Lynn thanked him and began signing donation checks that day. After several weeks, the local fire chief left her a message asking why the bank had not contributed to their annual spring carnival. Hurrying to find Arlen, she blurted, "I've made a terrible mistake. I forgot to budget for the fire department carnival, and the chief called. Can you call him back and explain?"*
>
> *"No, you need to call him," Arlen reminded her. "You can do it."*
>
> —*L.C.D.*

At some point, your employee or child may change; she may no longer share your commitment. You must accept this risk: she may make choices based on a value different from that of your organization or family. Nevertheless, you cannot control her choices, even if the situation becomes difficult for her or the outcome appears to reflect badly on you. Let go of any need to impose your values. You can only control how you respond.

> *Seventeen-year-old Jackson had always been an honor student. Now at the end of high school, he was in danger of failing his senior English class. His father, Myron, pointed out that Jackson was limiting his college opportunities by not working harder. Although Jackson acknowledged that this was probably true, he maintained that his senior year of high school was his last opportunity to spend time with the friends he had known since grade school. Myron valued academic excellence and could not imagine how Jackson could put friendship above school.*
>
> *"I'm not willing to give up planning the senior assembly, decorating for the prom, and going on our camping retreat. The end of high school is just too important to me, Dad. I'll try to keep up with my English, but I'm not missing any senior activities."*
>
> *Although disappointed, Myron chose to enjoy Jackson's last months at home and let Jackson experience the results of his choice.*
>
> — *C.C.M.*

As a mentor, you aim for mutual understanding to preserve your relationship when an employee or child rejects a value. You may want to fight back as though you have been personally attacked. However, because of your relationship, respect her right to a different perspective.

When you and your employee or child recognize conflicting values, respond by conferencing. The extent to which her value differs from yours predicts your response. On the one hand, you may accept her value; on the other hand, you may endanger the entire relationship because of extreme discrepancies between your values. The difference between her value of cooperation and your value of friendship may result in very little discussion; however, her value of independence and your value of teamwork may call for a more intense conference.

You may choose to respond to a conflicting value in one of the following ways. Consider these responses in numerical order for the least threat to your relationship.

Responding to Conflicting Values

1. **Choose your employee's or child's value.**

2. **Choose another common value.**

3. **Choose an expanded expectation that meets both values.**

4. **Choose to maintain the relationship.**

5. **Choose to endanger the relationship because of a higher value.**

1. Choose your employee's or child's value.

When you realize that your employee or child has adopted a different value, think before you react. Initially, you may want to force her to conform to your beliefs. Instead, listen to her point of view. *I know we need to make every sale, but our parts won't fit the customer's machine.* You may discover that her value reflects the beliefs of the organization or family more appropriately for the situation. *I'm late because I stopped to help some people in a car accident.*

When Dorothy flew from out of state to visit her married daughter and three young grandchildren, she was shocked that the kitchen was in disarray. "Kalina, how can you possibly let your kitchen floor go like this? Get your mop, and I'll clean it up, while you clean out that refrigerator."

Kalina explained to her mother, "I know my house isn't clean, but it is more important to me to spend time with the children. Would you help me read stories instead?"

"You're right," Dorothy agreed. "I made this trip because I wanted to spend time with all of you." Even though she liked a clean house, Dorothy accepted that reading stories to her grandchildren was a priority for Kalina and for herself as well.

— *C.C.M.*

2. Choose another common value.

Mentor managers and parents begin a conference by searching for points of agreement rather than discussing points of disagreement. *I was trying to be so thorough, and Anton kept rushing me. Finally, we realized that as long as we delivered the slides to the meeting by noon, the client would be happy.* Validating feelings will help you understand the other person's perspective and discover a possible common value. *Camille signed up for a daily aerobics class that ends at seven o'clock but was upset because I still served dinner at six-thirty. As we talked, I realized how hurt she was. We agreed that family dinners are important and rearranged our schedules.*

"I'm afraid I've really messed up," Edward, the county health department administrator told me. "Things have gone so far with Arlene. She is one of my best nurses, but I'm afraid I'm going to have to fire her." He explained that a few months earlier he had become concerned that Arlene often arrived three to five minutes late. Edward began standing by the time clock at eight each morning to "catch" her. Now, by strictly following the department's procedures, he had escalated to two letters of reprimand. One more and Arlene would be gone.

I asked Edward if this issue of three to five minutes' tardiness was the one he chose to lose her over, and he confessed that it was not. "But rules are rules, and timeliness is important," Edward lamented. I suggested that he conference with Arlene, asking for her feelings and suggestions.

A few days later, Edward called me to describe their meeting. "She was just as frustrated as I was," he sighed. "She and I both are concerned about our service to patients. We finally agreed that it was okay for her, and the other nurses, to arrive a few minutes late, as long as they were ready to see their first patients when the examination rooms fill up about five minutes after eight."

—L.C.D.

3. Choose an expanded expectation that meets both values.

If your conference reaches an impasse and you cannot find a common value, perhaps you can discover an expectation that satisfies both values. The same action by different people may represent two unrelated values. *I have always attended community activities because I enjoy being involved, but Temple just sees them as a networking opportunity. Oh well. As long as he goes, I'm happy.*

Eleanor was proud of her orderly house. She had raised her son, Hogan, to make his bed, hang up his clothes, and generally keep his room neat. When Hogan turned thirteen, Eleanor began to notice that his room was less and less orderly. When she asked him about it, Hogan replied, "It's just not important to me, Mom. I'm too busy!"

"It sounds like junior high life is pretty exciting," Eleanor began. "I think you know that it's important to me that the house is neat and organized. But I'm not willing to go into your room and clean it up when you know how to do it. What other options could we come up with?"

"Mom, I told you I'm just not into it anymore," Hogan snapped.

"I think what bothers me the most is when we have company, and they see the mess in your room," Eleanor mused.

"Okay, Mom, I'll just keep the door shut."

"Actually, Hogan, that sounds like a really good plan," Eleanor agreed.

—C.C.M.

Choosing values different from their parents often accompanies the learning process for teenagers. This difference of opinion does not reject your authority but indicates normal growth toward independent thought. *I almost died when Kirk came home with green hair! But then I told him how my parents felt when I pierced my ears. After our talk, Kirk offered to wear a cap when we go out to dinner together.* Within a mentoring relationship, a teenager's choice of contrary values generally proves temporary.

4. Choose to maintain the relationship.

When your conference fails to determine common values or expectations, you must make a crucial choice. Will you endanger your relationship over conflicting values? At work, sustaining your relationship in the midst of the organization's non-negotiable values may stretch the limits of your interpersonal skills. *Estelle, it would be great for you to stay home with the baby part-time, but all of our positions require full-time attention. If you decide that staying home is more important, let's keep in touch and talk again when the baby is older.* At home, your unconditional parental love may cause you to wrestle over such a predicament. *When Price left home after we didn't approve of his girlfriend, at first I didn't want to talk to him. But after I thought about it, I realized that my love for him is more important than fighting over his girlfriend.*

> *Sherman hated turning in weekly sales reports because he valued the autonomy of his outside sales position at the radio station. "It's nobody's business where I go or who I call on as long as I make sales."*
>
> *Leona, the sales manager, asked Sherman to conference about his sales calls. "Sherman, communicating with each other about sales prospects is a key to our whole sales team's success. I can tell you have strong feelings about turning in sales reports. Is the Friday afternoon deadline something we could adjust for you?"*
>
> *"No, I don't care when the deadline is. I'll just try harder."*

"Thanks," Leona said, as Sherman stood to leave. "Turning in the reports is a definite requirement for employment here."

At 4:30 the next Friday afternoon, Sherman appeared in Leona's doorway, with the contents of his desk in a box under his arm. "Well, I'm firing myself," he explained. "I'm not going to do those reports, so I might as well go."

"I'm sorry you feel that way, Sherman," Leona said, coming around her desk to shake his hand. "You're a good salesman, and I hate to lose you. Keep in touch with us, won't you?"

Months later, Sherman called Leona from his new job at a competitive station. "You sure woke me up," he told her. "Every sales job I looked for required reports, so I settled for a different job." They visited for a while, laughed about his "firing himself," and agreed to meet for lunch sometime soon.

———*—L.C.D.*

5. Choose to endanger the relationship because of a higher value.

Occasionally, an employee or child makes a choice that violates a fundamental value, such as health, safety, or respect. She may even choose to break a law or harm herself or others. Although maintaining the relationship has always been your goal, at this point you consciously hold to a higher value. *Wendell, I ran into your former university department head at the conference, and he said you never actually completed your graduate degree. We cannot let you counsel people anymore.*

Sully asked me to coach a long-term employee of the auto dealership. "Blythe works really hard in the office, but she is quite difficult to get along with. She is rude to anybody who asks her a question, and she makes you feel uncomfortable when you walk into the office," he explained. "We feel like we owe it to her to have you work with her, but as many times as we've talked with her, we have our doubts."

After Blythe and I met several times, she called me. "This is a waste of time," she complained. "I'm not coming to see you again, and if they don't want to take me like I am, then that's too bad!"

I reported this to Sully, and the next day he called to tell me that he had let Blythe go. "She just couldn't understand how important a pleasant, cooperative environment is to us."

—*L.C.D.*

You may agonize about what could happen as a result of a choice made by an employee or child and feel compelled to intervene. However, your determination to uphold a basic value of the organization or family has the potential to damage your relationship irreparably.

I recently heard the story of a grandmother whose teenage granddaughter visited for part of the summer. She smelled vomit each time she went in the granddaughter's bathroom and began to suspect bulimia. The grandmother gave a great deal of thought to how to tell her own daughter, a single parent, of her observation.

Finally, she decided to explain that the granddaughter's visit had given them an opportunity to spend a lot of time together. As a result, she suspected a health problem. The grandmother risked alienating both her daughter and her granddaughter by sharing her suspicion, but her overriding concern for her granddaughter's health gave her the needed courage.

— *C.C.M.*

Potentially alienating your employee or child presents one of the most difficult decisions you may ever make. *When I heard the description of the arsonist on the news, my fears that it could be my own son were realized. I knew I had to call the police if he was not willing to turn himself in.* When you let go of the need to impose your values on your employee or child, you accept the risk that she might choose a conflicting value. At this point, you can only control how you respond as the two of you conference.

The examples and worksheets on the following pages will help you practice your responses. Remember that the farther down the list of responses you go, the more you jeopardize your relationship.

RESPONDING TO CONFLICTING VALUES AT WORK EXAMPLE

Your expectation: *Petty cash is for office-related emergencies.*

Your value: *Honesty*

Employee's expectation: *I can pay for my lunches from petty cash.*

Employee's value: *Expediency*

Answer the questions in numerical order. Stop when you arrive at a YES response, and Let Go.

1. Do your values agree?
   ☐ Yes   ☒ No

2. Can you choose your employee's value?
   ☐ Yes   ☒ No

3. Can you choose another common value?
   ☐ Yes   ☒ No

4. Can you choose an expanded expectation that meets both values?
   ☐ Yes   ☒ No

5. Can you choose to maintain the relationship over any other value?
   ☐ Yes   ☒ No

If no, take action and endanger the relationship.
Under no circumstances can you take money from petty cash for personal expenses.

RESPONDING TO CONFLICTING VALUES AT HOME EXAMPLE

Your expectation: *Melcia must practice daily to learn how to play the piano.*

Your value: *Artistic expression*

Child's expectation: *I like to play the piano, but I don't like to practice every day.*

Child's value: *Flexibility*

Answer the questions in numerical order. Stop when you arrive at a YES response, and Let Go.

1. Do your values agree?
   ☐ Yes   ☒ No

2. Can you choose your child's value?
   ☐ Yes   ☒ No

3. Can you choose another common value?
   ☐ Yes   ☒ No

4. Can you choose an expanded expectation that meets both values?
   ☒ Yes   ☐ No
   Melcia can still take lessons and enjoy playing the piano, even if she doesn't practice regularly.

5. Can you choose to maintain the relationship over any other value?
   ☐ Yes   ☐ No

If no, take action and endanger the relationship.

RESPONDING TO CONFLICTING VALUES AT WORK PRACTICE

Your expectation: _____

Your value: _____

Employee's expectation: _____

Employee's value: _____

Answer the questions in numerical order. Stop when you arrive at a YES response, and Let Go.

1. Do your values agree?
   ☐ Yes ☐ No

2. Can you choose your employee's value?
   ☐ Yes ☐ No

3. Can you choose another common value?
   ☐ Yes ☐ No

4. Can you choose an expanded expectation that meets both values?
   ☐ Yes ☐ No

5. Can you choose to maintain the relationship over any other value?
   ☐ Yes ☐ No

If no, take action and endanger the relationship.

RESPONDING TO CONFLICTING VALUES AT HOME PRACTICE

Your expectation: _____

Your value: _____

Child's expectation: _____

Child's value: _____

Answer the questions in numerical order. Stop when you arrive at a YES response, and Let Go.

1. Do your values agree?
   ☐ Yes   ☐ No

2. Can you choose your employee's value?
   ☐ Yes   ☐ No

3. Can you choose another common value?
   ☐ Yes   ☐ No

4. Can you choose an expanded expectation that meets both values?
   ☐ Yes   ☐ No

5. Can you choose to maintain the relationship over any other value?
   ☐ Yes   ☐ No

If no, take action and endanger the relationship.

Letting Go Skill: Maintain the Relationship

Your guidance and encouragement have greatly influenced your employee or child to become responsible and self-directed. He has the confidence and ability to set and achieve his own goals. Even though he experiences the natural result of his decisions, you offer encouragement and support, listen to his concerns, celebrate when he succeeds, and empathize when he fails.

When I was a little girl in Norman, Oklahoma, and learned that China was on the other side of the world, I dreamed how exciting it would be to dig a tunnel all the way through the earth. Wouldn't the Chinese people be surprised when I popped out? I found a corner of our backyard and started digging. Before long, the neighborhood children had joined in my mission to "dig to China."

After several long days of digging, I began to realize that there was a possibility that digging to China might be too much of an undertaking for my little group of diggers. I had a cousin in Oklahoma City, only twenty miles away. Wouldn't he be surprised when I popped out in his backyard? We renewed our digging, convinced that soon we would be in Oklahoma City.

It wasn't long before it dawned on me that it was going to take a long time to actually dig to my cousin's house. Revising our mission one more time, I was able to get my friends to recommit by promising an underground clubhouse if we would just keep digging for a few more days. With renewed hope, we kept shoveling as we imagined a secret door leading to an underground room.

As our little arms grew weary and our efforts had only produced a plot of overturned soil, the neighborhood children began to straggle off, one by one. Still determined, I kept digging as my parents watched and silently supported my efforts. That night when darkness prevented me from working anymore, I came inside almost ready to admit defeat. There on the kitchen counter was a package of radish seeds.

— *C.C.M.*

Mentoring always aims toward building a relationship with your employee or child. Connecting through shared experiences, you discover closeness and trust. You care about each other, value differing opinions, and create a respectful partnership.

At work, the quality of your relationship, though professional, keeps the workplace energized. As a mentor manager, you show your consideration, respect, and trust every day. Now you find that your employee offers those to you in return. Your supportive relationship takes advantage of mutual strengths, and the workplace prospers.

Vernon was an engineer who should never have been a supervisor. He enjoyed his work but avoided interacting with employees. I was hired to coach Vernon's supervisory skills because his manager realized that the engineering firm had asked a loyal employee and a good engineer to go beyond his personal strengths.

"I really don't like management, but I don't want to let the firm down," Vernon told me after six months of coaching. He had completed every assignment and worked to improve his skills. He even shared his readings with his wife. But the more he tried, the more he and I became convinced that managing others was not for him. Together, we went to his manager, explained his dilemma, and worked out a lateral transfer to an engineering position with no supervisory duties. Everyone was pleased.

Two years later, a handwritten note from Vernon told me that he had a brain tumor. "Before my health fails, I want to let you know how much you helped me. You showed me a way to 'save face' at work and to have more time with my family. I also learned a lot, even though I don't want to practice it. Thanks for caring."

—*L.C.D.*

At home, the warmth and openness that you share define your family. You enjoy similar activities, laugh at the same things, and feel safe to disclose your vulnerabilities. You help each other and work together proactively to avoid problems. As a mentor parent, your interest and appreciation give your child a sense of security and make your home a welcoming retreat. Relationships draw your children home.

> *When I was a young mother with a new baby and a preschooler, my parents flew to Seattle to visit our family. Driving them home from the airport, I apologized for the condition our home would be in when we arrived. "The baby has been sick, and things have been so busy. I didn't even have time to vacuum."*
>
> *When we walked in the door, my father took off his coat and tie. As he rolled up the sleeves of his starched white shirt he asked, "Where do you keep your vacuum cleaner?"*
>
> *Twenty minutes later, my father had vacuumed our carpet. He put away the vacuum and rolled down his sleeves. "Now," he smiled. "Let's sit down and enjoy your children."*
>
> —— *C.C.M.*

You may feel more successful or satisfied in one of your mentoring roles than in the other. At work, the position itself, the salary, and management training may contribute to your confidence as a manager, while at home, the intensity of a twenty-four-hour job without paid holidays or even private bathroom breaks, leaves you frazzled. Or, you may find the internal satisfaction at home of sticky kisses, lunch in the park and casual dress more satisfying than the hurried pace of business meetings and stressful deadlines. You may choose one mentoring role over the other for a time in your life or balance them both indefinitely. However, whether you choose *Where's my teddy bear?* or *Where's my time card?* the strategies and skills you exhibit as a mentor will enrich the lives of all those you influence.

My life in the sixth grade was fairly typical of other preadolescent girls, including giggling about "boyfriends" and shifting allegiances among each other. One of our classmates, Ana Smith, came from a poor home in the country. The rest of us, with our self-absorbed ways of thinking, never thought to invite Ana to our slumber parties or include her in our playground secrets.

One day our class was going on a field trip. My mother had volunteered to drive, and when I saw the list of girls assigned to our car, I was mortified to see that Ana was among them. Piling in the car and teasing each other about our "boyfriends," we ignored Ana.

After a few minutes, my mother interrupted, "So, Ana, do you have a boyfriend?"

Immediately, there was quiet. Ana smiled and murmured, "Yes, ma'am."

That day stands out as a turning point in my life, when my mother taught me a great lesson about humanity and compassion.

— *C.C.M.*

All relationships have high and low points, good and bad days. Yet, a relationship overlooks an employee's angry retort and forgives a child for forgetting lunch money. The bond you develop in a mentoring relationship proves stronger than momentary disagreements or disappointments.

Frustrated with nine-year-old Roberto's behavior, his mother said, "I'm going to go see a counselor about your behavior. I am at the end of my rope!"

Roberto replied, "You should talk to the counselor about getting more rope."

— *C.C.M.*

As a mentor, you try to model how to express emotions appropriately. Venting anger and frustration can destroy months of building trust. You owe it to the relationship to plan how you will discuss a sensitive issue. At work, you might take an item off an agenda until you talk with your employee privately. At home, you model and teach getting distance, cooling down, or needing privacy. Your child learns relationship skills through his relationship with you.

Kerry was grocery shopping with four-year-old Leanna and two-year-old Davy piled into the shopping cart. Having learned to give the children something to keep them busy while she shopped, Kerry asked Leanna, "How many chicken teriyaki sticks would you like from the deli?"

"Two," Leanna replied.

Kerry purchased two chicken teriyaki sticks for Leanna and also got one for her brother. Returning to the cart, she first handed a stick to Davy.

Leanna immediately started screaming at the top of her lungs, assuming that Davy had just gotten one of her two chicken teriyaki sticks. Kerry couldn't figure out what was wrong and stared at Leanna, momentarily unsure what to do.

"Privacy!" screamed Leanna. "I need privacy!"

Kerry realized at once that she had taught Leanna to go somewhere private when she was upset. Looking around the crowded supermarket, she wondered what she could possibly do. Meanwhile, Leanna continued to yell, "Privacy! I want privacy!"

Kerry lifted Leanna from the cart and carried her to a nearby women's restroom. Gently putting her inside for "privacy," Kerry stood guard at the door. After a few minutes, Leanna had stopped screaming. When Kerry entered the restroom, she saw a composed Leanna washing her hands and two teriyaki sticks floating in the toilet.

—*C.C.M.*

Mentoring relationships can provide delight and companionship, as your employee or child becomes a person with whom you can laugh and have fun. Developing your own sense of humor helps your employee or child to see humor in the ordinary as well. Employees enjoy retelling about *making banana splits in the lobby on Friday afternoon.* Families laughingly remember *the time we tried to move the box springs up the stairs.*

> *Pete, the bank president, was admired and respected by his staff and his customers. He was willing to dress up like a leprechaun for a week, take his turn cleaning the lunchroom dishes, and help an employee team deliver cast-off bank furniture to a less fortunate family. His employees loved his infectious laugh and the "Donald Duck" voice he used with children. When he called customers whose accounts were overdrawn, his standard explanation was that they were "underdeposited."*
>
> —*L.C.D.*

Rituals reflect values and celebrate relationships. What do you do in your organization or family to celebrate together? As a mentor, enjoy creating shared memories. At work, celebrate with more than a token turkey and an obligatory company picnic. Share of yourself with tomatoes from your garden, a favorite book, or a convention souvenir for an employee's child. Involve employees in community activities, not for the recognition but for the joy of giving and working together. At home, take your child for ice cream after your errands simply to enjoy time with him rather than to reward him for good behavior. Let him light candles for a candlelight dinner. Decorate the front door to celebrate family successes or spend New Year's Day putting family photos in albums.

> *It was late October, and the smell of chili filled the hospital. The senior management team was cooking and serving "lunch" for all three shifts. Glenda, the nursing coordinator, was Little Red Riding Hood; Raymond, the financial vice president, was a blue robot with a lighted*

chest; and Lillian, from the business office, who was pregnant, was dressed like a pea pod. They laughed with the employees who came through the line, posed for pictures, and took the good-natured kidding about how sleepy they would be the next day.

But the best costume award went to Malcolm, the CEO, who dressed like a bunch of grapes, completely covered with a green body stocking and green balloons. He kept popping his balloons on the hot chili pot and having to blow up new ones between shifts.

—*L.C.D.*

A mentor can have no greater honor than to participate in the personal growth of an employee or child, whether for a few months or a lifetime. A parent who invested time and energy in mentoring thoughtfully reflected *It is harder to live life like we were than it is to mentor. It is so much harder; people just don't realize that. You feel so much better when you focus on your relationship.*

When he called me for lunch, I had no idea that it would change my life. Larry had been the chief operations officer of a municipal ambulance service for which I had trained and coached managers for six years. In addition to his offbeat sense of humor, he was an excellent delegator and easily recognized potential in others, even when they did not see it in themselves.

"I'm dying," he said matter-of-factly. "I don't have long, and I have two requests of you. I want you to see that my living will is enforced, no heroic efforts. And I want you to present my eulogy. But, I want you to make people laugh and celebrate my life."

I was stunned. At first, I just nodded, but when I caught my breath, I told him how honored I was, "Those are not requests anyone can turn down."

Over the next few months, we met often over lunch, eventually at his home, and finally in the hospital. We discussed life, food, and politics, but never what I would say when he was gone. He told me that Vonda, the service's financial officer, would handle all his finances and that he had instructed her to spare no expense on his behalf.

Too soon, Vonda and I were making funeral arrangements. As we left the church, we looked at the hotel across the street and had an inspiration. I will always believe it came straight from Larry: we booked a reception with food, flowers, and music, to follow the funeral service.

Even though I lost my composure twice, I managed to have those at Larry's funeral laughing at our memories of such a unique person. It was with pleasure, at the conclusion of my remarks, that I invited everyone to a reception across the street to celebrate the life of our friend.

—*L.C.D.*

Connecting the Mentoring Model: Letting Go and Conferencing

Letting go represents a turning point in your relationship with your employee or child. She has demonstrated her ability to take initiative, consistent with the values of your organization or family. Now, you recognize her readiness to make responsible choices, and you prepare to shift control exclusively to her.

RELATIONSHIPS

Letting Go
Confirm Readiness
Accept the Risk
Maintain the Relationship

Conferencing
Validate Feelings
Invite an Alternative
Aim for Consensus

Throughout your ongoing relationship with your employee or child, you naturally and periodically return to conferencing when she encounters new situations and seeks your input. *I'm having trouble with the design of this new brochure. What can I do to give it a different look?* When you share the same values, your conference becomes a collaborative problem-solving conversation that validates your mutual feelings and agreement. *The neighbors haven't paid me for mowing their lawn last month. Do you think it would be okay for me to ask them about it again?*

> *"Mom, I need help!" twenty-three-year old Ashley said on the telephone. "My car tag expires next week, and I can't find the title. Do you have it?"*
>
> *"I don't think so, Honey," her mother replied. "I think it was in that box of your things that we sent after you moved out of state."*
>
> *"I don't want to drive with an expired tag. How can I get a new title?" Ashley asked.*
>
> *"I agree. Let's see. Your title is from this state . . . ."*
>
> *"Oh, that's right," Ashley realized. "Can the tag agency fax me the form I need?"*
>
> *"Sure, I'll call and give them your fax number."*
>
> *"Thanks, Mom. Hey, how did your cake turn out on Sunday?"*
> ———————————————————————————————*C.C.M.*

You also return to conferencing if your employee or child shares your values but begins to make independent choices that seem inappropriate. *I heard you ask your team to select a caterer, but then you hired a different one. You must really like the one you selected. How do you think your team will react to your decision?* Collaborate to help her discover alternatives that reflect your shared value. *I can understand why you decided to go to the mall after school. But your little brother was really disappointed that you didn't come home to play with him like you promised. I know you didn't mean to hurt his feelings. How can you make it up to him?*

Ultimately, you respond with a conference when your employee or child makes an independent choice that conflicts with your value. Focus this conversation on values and aim for understanding rather than agreement. *Your decision to discontinue the public's use of our conference room will make our office quieter, but it will leave many community groups with no meeting place. Help me understand how you arrived at your decision.* However, you can return to conferencing about conflicting values only once without being accused of nagging. *I know you like to play golf on Saturday afternoons even when it is your weekend to have the children, but I worry that they don't get enough of your attention since the divorce.*

Carla, the deputy director of a state agency, valued honesty and tact, as well as respect for a leader's position. Her memos and discussions with Baldwin, the director, were always straightforward but carefully crafted to have a positive tone. However, Lois, one of Carla's division managers, valued absolute candor that spared no one.

One afternoon Baldwin confided in Carla that he was quite disappointed with the tone of Lois's last few memos, "She doesn't think through what she says and focuses on problems instead of solutions."

Carla thought about his comments for a few days and weighed her obligation to Lois. Since their first few months together, Carla had trusted Lois as a competent manager and had rarely interfered with her choices. But this situation could damage Lois's career.

Over lunch, Carla brought up the subject of Lois's memos. "You know, I'm certain that your intent is to keep Baldwin informed, but when you tell him everything that is wrong he may think you can't find a solution."

"No, I'm just trying to give him all the facts. I don't know what else he wants."

"It's a difficult situation. Is there any other way you could address issues to him?" Carla prompted.

"No, I think he should have all the facts about a situation. I can't communicate with him in any other way."

"You sound pretty sure. At least you know how he'll react. If you want to bounce any ideas off of me, I'll be glad to listen," Carla concluded.

———————————————————————————————*—L.C.D.*

Of all three connections between strategies in the mentoring model, the connection between letting go and conferencing has the greatest potential for serious damage to your relationship. You may feel betrayed when your employee or child makes independent choices that do not reflect your values, and she may feel challenged when you question her judgement. However, conferencing offers the best chance to preserve your relationship.

Trina's mother came to counseling to "find a strong enough consequence to keep Trina home." On Saturday, eighteen-year-old Trina had taken the bus from her suburban home into the city and had not returned until late that night. "She won't tell me where she is going or when she will be home! And when I ask her, she says it is none of my business. What if next weekend she decides to take a bus to New York City?"

"She might," I agreed. "But if you talk to her about how much you love her and your concern for her safety, maybe she'll understand why knowing that she is okay is important to you."

The next week Trina's mom reported, "I sat down with her and told her that I understand her need for independence and that I love her and worry about her when she just takes off on the bus. I didn't talk about consequences but told her that I just want to know that she is okay. Then last Saturday she told me that she was taking the bus into the city for shopping and dinner with a friend and voluntarily said she would be home by eleven-thirty."

"And what happened?" I asked.

"I couldn't believe it! I heard the front door open at eleven-twenty-eight!"

———————————————————————————————*—C.C.M.*

Connecting the Entire Mentoring Model

The mentoring model represents the entire mentoring process, rooted in the values of your organization or family and leading to supportive, respectful relationships. It connects the strategies and skills that effective managers and parents use to encourage motivation and initiative in employees and children. These interrelated strategies enable you to adapt with confidence to any situation at work or at home. As a mentor, you move up the model from strategy to strategy in response to an employee's or child's readiness to accept more responsibility; you move down in response to his need for more direction.

You can employ mentoring strategies simultaneously as you respond to the skills and abilities of your employee or child. With an employee, you might structure about the value of promptness, coach about how to create a spreadsheet, conference about his extra long lunch hours and let go of his trustworthy communication with customers—all on the same day.

With your ten-year-old, you might structure about why the dog needs fresh water, coach about how to determine the time of a Saturday matinee, conference about what he does with his friends after the movie, and let go of his responsible decision to eat a healthy breakfast—all before he gets dressed in the morning.

Throughout your mentoring relationship, you trust in the potential of your employees and children to develop responsibility and self-direction. As a mentor manager or mentor parent, you build supportive and successful relationships at work and at home.

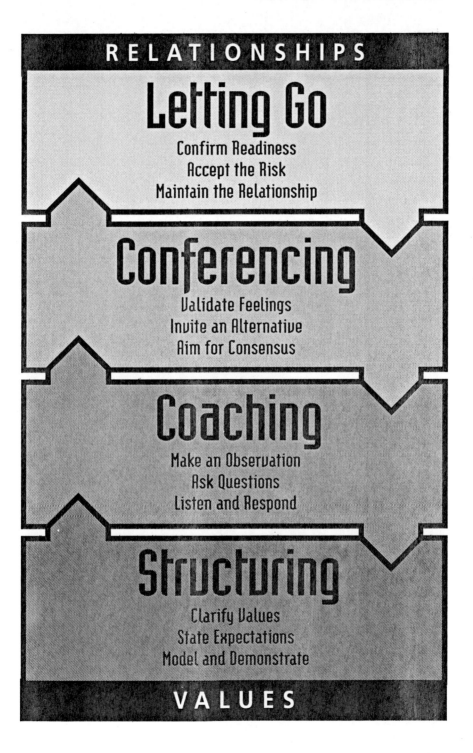

RELATIONSHIPS

Letting Go
Confirm Readiness
Accept the Risk
Maintain the Relationship

Conferencing
Validate Feelings
Invite an Alternative
Aim for Consensus

Coaching
Make an Observation
Ask Questions
Listen and Respond

Structuring
Clarify Values
State Expectations
Model and Demonstrate

VALUES

ABOUT THE AUTHORS

Linda Culp Dowling

Linda Culp Dowling is a management coach, communication skills trainer, and an organizational development consultant. She founded Communication Concepts, a training and development firm, in 1979, after fifteen years in broadcast management and education. She serves clients in business, education, government, manufacturing, and healthcare. A native Oklahoman, she holds a B.A. in Mass Communication from Wayne State University in Detroit and taught management and communication courses at the University of Oklahoma. She is a member of the American Society for Training and Development and teaches in the OU Training and Development Certification Program. Linda is featured in a training video, *Coaching and Performance Feedback Training Scenes,* produced by Quality Media Resources of Seattle. She and her husband, Pete, live at Falconhead Resort and Country Club in southern Oklahoma and enjoy traveling with friends and spending time with their children and grandchildren.

Cecile Culp Mielenz

Cecile Culp Mielenz joined the parent education faculty of Shoreline Community College in Seattle, Washington, in 1982, after five years in university teaching and administration. In conjunction with her college responsibilities, she directs a parent cooperative preschool, where she works with 85 parent volunteers each year. Collaboratively, they operate Woodinville Family Preschool. As a child development consultant, Cecile contracts with the Bureau of Education and Research. Through BER she presents seminars to early childhood teachers throughout the United States and Canada, for which she received an Outstanding National Educator award in

234

2001. In addition, Cecile maintains a private counseling practice devoted to parents. Her M.S. and Ph.D. degrees from Florida State University are in Child Development. Cecile and her husband, Mike, are the parents of two daughters and live in the Seattle area. They enjoy gardening, ethnic foods, and living in the Pacific Northwest.

Four Easy Ways to Order More Copies of Mentor Manager, Mentor Parent!

1. **VISIT OUR WEBSITE** www.mentormanagermentorparent.com to order additional books or to request information about our consulting services or seminar presentations.

2. **MAIL** the order form on the next page along with your check payable to *ComCon Books* or your credit card information to:

    ComCon Books
    904 Cimarron Circle
    Burneyville, OK 73430

3. **FAX** the order form along with your credit card information to 580-276-2590.

4. **CALL 1-888-606-7130** toll free, and have your credit card ready.

MENTOR MANAGER, MENTOR PARENT - ORDER FORM

(PLEASE PRINT)

NAME			
ADDRESS			
CITY		STATE	ZIP
HOME PHONE	WORK PHONE		
EMAIL ADDRESS			

PLEASE CHARGE MY ☐ Visa ☐ MasterCard

NAME ON CARD	
CARD NUMBER	EXP. / /

PLEASE SEND ME

NUMBER OF BOOKS	=	_____
$19.95 US / $31.95 CAN per book	X $	_____
SUBTOTAL	= $	_____
SHIPPING & TAX (per book)	+ $	_____

Oklahoma residents $ 4.50 Shipping and Tax
Washington residents $ 5.00 Shipping and Tax
All other states $ 3.00 Shipping Only
Canadian residents $ 5.00 (CAN) Shipping Only

TOTAL	= $	_____

Thank you for your order!

Printed in the United States
1322600007B/58-81